Physical Characteristics of the Dandie Dinmont Terrier

(from the American Kennel Club breed standard)

Body: Long, strong and flexible. Ribs are well sprung and well rounded. The chest is well developed and well let down between the forelegs. The underline reflects the curves of the topline.

Topline: Rather low at the shoulder, having a slight downward curve and a corresponding arch over the loins, with a very slight gradual drop from the top of the loins to the root of the tail.

Hindquarters: Hind legs are a little longer than the forelegs and are set rather wide apart, but not spread out in an unnatural manner. The upper and lower thighs are rounded and muscular and approximately the same length; stifles angulated, in balance with forequarters. The hocks are well let down and rear pasterns perpendicular to the ground.

Coat: The hair should be about 2 inches long; the body coat is a mixture of about two-thirds hardish hair with about one-third soft hair, giving a sort of crisp texture.

Height: From 8 to 11 inches at the top of the shoulders. Length from top of shoulders to root of tail is 1 to 2 inches less than twice the height.

Rear feet: Much smaller than the front feet.

Dandie Dinmont Terrier

By Betty-Anne Stenmark

Contents

Training Your Dandie Dinmont Terrier   **107**

Learn the principles of house-training the Dandie Dinmont Terrier, including the use of crates and basic scent instincts. Get started by introducing the pup to his collar and leash and progress to the basic obedience commands: sit, come, stay and heel.

Healthcare of Your Dandie Dinmont Terrier   **121**

By Lowell Ackerman DVM, DACVD
Become your dog's healthcare advocate and a well-educated canine keeper. Select a skilled and able veterinarian. Discuss vaccinations and infectious diseases, the neuter/spay decision and parasite control.

Showing Your Dandie Dinmont Terrier   **132**

Learn how to get started in AKC shows, how they are organized and what's required for your dog to become a champion. Discuss the specific steps to train a puppy for the ring. Take a leap into the realms of obedience trials, agility, earthdog events and tracking tests.

KENNEL CLUB BOOKS® DANDIE DINMONT TERRIER
ISBN: 1-59378-271-3

Copyright © 2006 • Kennel Club Books, LLC • 308 Main Street, Allenhurst, NJ 07711 USA
Cover Design Patented: US 6,435,559 B2 • Printed in South Korea

Library of Congress Cataloging-in-Publication Data
Stenmark, Betty-Anne.
Dandie Dinmont terrier / by Betty-Anne Stenmark.
  p. cm.
ISBN 1-59378-271-3
1. Dandie Dinmont terrier. I. Title.
SF429.D33S74 2006
636.755--dc22   2006012318

10 9 8 7 6 5 4 3 2 1

Photography by Alice van Kempen
with additional photography by:

Allen Photography, Animal Pics, Ashbey Photography, Backstage Photography, Carol Beuchat, Mary Bloom, Booth Photography, Tom Bruni, Callea Photo, Carolina Biological Supply, Paul Cavalt, Cook Photography, John W. Davies, Jr., Isabelle Francais, Pamela Gelme, William P. Gilbert Photography, Gay Glazbrook, Tim Golden, Dr. Emma Greenway, Chris Halvorson, Wallace Heaton Ltd., Holloway Studios, Tom Johnson Photography, Jansken Photography, Bernard W. Kernan Show Dog Photography, Steven D. Newell, Tam C. Nguyen, Perry Phillips , Don Petrulis Photography, Pix 'n Pages, Joe Rinehart Photo, Ritter Photography, Kitten Rodwell, Evelyn M. Shafer, Sportphotography.ca, Sally Stasytis (Challenge Photos), Roy and Betty-Anne Stenmark, Winning Images and Peg Ziebart.

Illustrations by Heidi B. Martin.

DEDICATION

To my husband Roy, who has supported and encouraged me all these years in my pursuit of breeding better Dandies. In recent years he has prefaced many of his suggestions with, "If you insist on continuing to breed Dandies I would breed this bitch to that dog." Some were very good suggestions!

This book also honors our original three Dandies who spurred our devotion to the breed. They were our foundation bitches, three mustards: Bess, her daughter, Allspice, and her granddaughter, Ginger. These dogs can be found seven and eight generations back in our pedigrees today.

I must also honor the more recent contributions of two young women who deserve much of the credit for the current success of King's Mtn. They are Sandra Pretari of San Bruno, California and Emma Greenway of Jollygaze Dandies in Victoria, Australia, who has generously shared her bloodlines with us. Sandra and Emma together have raised the bar with their expertise in grooming, training and presentation of our Dandies.

I must also thank Richard Beauchamp, whose introduction to the world of writing within the pure-bred dog community has led to this book, as well as numerous others. His guidance and encouragement are treasured.

DANDIE DINMONT TERRIER

The Dandie originated in the Border country between Scotland and England. They were first known as Mustard and Pepper Terriers, and the first writings about them date back to about 1700.

About the mid-1700s in the British Isles two distinct types of terriers were identified. One was a rough-coated, short-legged, long-backed dog, very strong and most commonly of a black or yellowish color mixed with white. The other was smooth-haired, shorter-bodied and more sprightly in appearance, generally of a reddish brown color or black with tan legs. Both types were great foes of all vermin and often successfully faced the fierce badger.

During this same period in the Border Counties of Northumberland, Cumberland, Westmoreland and Durham roamed tribes of gypsies, tinkers and musicians who bred their nameless terriers for work on fox, badger, otter, polecat, wildcat and marten, as well as for ratting and poaching. When the Faas, Allens, Andersons and Cammells gathered once or twice a year, the revelries included badger-baiting, dog-fighting and other contests designed to test the gameness of their individual terrier strains. The rivalry was keen, the liquor strong—and most such meetings ended in a brawl.

However, from these contests were chosen the outstanding dogs to be used for breeding. Little did these pioneers realize that one day this process would be known as selective breeding for particular traits.

William Allen (1704–1779), a bagpiper known usually as "Piper" Allen, had what many thought to be a most pure strain of Mustard and Pepper Terriers. He chose to keep his strain to himself and was not interested in selling puppies but preferred to occasionally use them as barter, giving a puppy in exchange for a favor. James Davidson, a tenant farmer in Hindlee, was lucky to acquire a breeding pair from Piper Allen. Later, Mr. Davidson was recognized as one of the early successful breeders and found himself the model for a character in the popular early 19th century novel written by Sir Walter

The Dandie Dinmont Terrier, originally known as the Mustard and Pepper Terrier, garnered its new name from a popular novel by Sir Walter Scott.

From a print in the early 1800s, Dandie Dinmont is shown with his terriers.

In 1897 the Dandie Dinmont was depicted in this painting by Arthur Wardle. The mustard-colored dog was Eng. Ch. Blacket House Yet and the pepper-colored dog was Eng. Ch. Ancrum Fanny. This painting has appeared in several books and is the property of Mrs. Lloyd Rayner.

Scott entitled *Guy Mannering*. The character patterned after Mr. Davidson was named Dandie Dinmont, and he kept dogs known as Mustard and Pepper Terriers. The novel was wildly popular at the time, and that popularity served to promote the breed.

The Mustard and Pepper Terriers had several different names through the early years, most often named after the farm whose owner was breeding them, such as Catcleugh Terriers and Hindlee Terriers. But certainly the final name, Dandie Dinmont Terrier, came from the

novel, and thus the Dandie is the only breed of dog whose name has a literary origin.

The foundation stock of the Mustard and Peppers, like many other breeds, is unknown although there are several theories about its origins. One that makes good sense is that they were the result of chance or the product of selection *à la* Darwin, the law that "like begets like" and ultimately the fixing of type. This is exactly what Piper Allen and his gypsy friends were doing when they chose to breed only from the contest winners. But from which dogs were these selections made? Some long-time Dandie fanciers will tell you it's a breed that looks like it was put together by a committee of Englishmen. True enough!

In Charles Cook's book of 1875, the earliest breed book published, *The Dandie Dinmont Terrier*, he referred to Stonehenge (J. M. Walsh), writing that the Dandie was a result of an original cross between an old Scotch Terrier, not to be confused with the modern Scottish Terrier, and the Welsh Harrier, sometimes called an Otterhound. The argument to support this theory is the somewhat houndy carriage of the Dandie's stern (tail) and the shape and set-on of his ears. The tail on both the Dandie and the Otterhound is carried in the shape of a scimitar, and they also share a common coat texture. In John Gordon's *The Dandie Dinmont Terrier Handbook* (first published in 1959), there is an engraving of an Otter Terrier dated 1846. This dog certainly appears that he could have been bred down from an Otterhound. Gordon goes on to claim that the large Dandies who weighed 24 pounds or more were the result of crosses between the original Mustard and Peppers with a large rough-haired Otter Terrier, but the results were not true Dandies.

That such crosses occurred is furthered by the Hound/Terrier cross from which the Bedlington Terrier almost certainly came. We are quite certain that in the beginning the Bedlington and the Dandie were closely related. The names Phoebe and Peachem figure prominently in early writings about both breeds. The Earl of Antrim in the late 1870s is said to have won prizes in both the Dandie Dinmont

Paul Scott of Tedburgh was known as one of the early pioneers of the Dandie Dinmont breed.

THE LEGENDARY DANDIE

The Dandie's gameness is legendary. In Sir Walter Scott's *Guy Mannering* he describes the Dandie's character with the lines: "...I have six terriers at home, forbye two couple of slowhunds, five grews, and a wheen other dogs. There's auld Pepper and auld Mustard, and young Pepper and young Mustard, and little Pepper and little Mustard - I had them a' regularly entered, first wi' rottens - then wi' stots or weasels - and then wi' the tods and brocks - and now they fear naething that ever cam' wi' a hairy skin on't." *Guy Mannering* most definitely would not be categorized as a "quick read" today. In order to understand the above quote, you would benefit from knowing that "rottens" were rats, "stots" weasels, "tods" foxes and "brocks" badgers.

and Bedlington Terrier classes at the same show with littermates! This theory has some credence as there are puppies born in occasional Dandie litters today who are high on leg, narrow in body, with narrow skulls, little stop and long muzzles and soft coats, appearing quite like the Bedlington.

Others thought there was also a dash of Bulldog thrown into this mix. Etchings of the Otterhound and the Bulldog from the period 1850–1875 show this is a possibility. Some modern fanciers feel the Bulldog theory has some merit, especially when the first

Dandie standard asked for, "forelegs short, with immense muscular development and bone, set wide apart…" Some of our senior judges still look for the Dandie to be wider in front than most of the modern-day breeders would purposefully select for today. And certainly the tenacity of the Bulldog would be widely coveted by the early breeders who were farmers and hunters. Don't confuse today's shorter, heavier Bulldog with the leaner, more agile Bulldog of 1850. There are great structural differences between them.

Stonehenge is also credited with the theory that the Dandie originated from this rough-haired borderland terrier crossed with a Dachshund. In *Dogs of the British Isles* (1882) he states that foreign stock was introduced to the native Scotch Terrier by itinerant gypsies from the Continent. This premise was supported by D. J. Thompson Gray, author of *The Dogs of Scotland* (1891), who claimed the Dandie's eye was more typical of the Dachshund's than any indigenous terrier breed, and also that the ears of many specimens of his day more resembled those of the Dachshund than any other breed. Charles Cook and other long-time Dandie breeders around 1875 very much disagreed with the Dachshund theory.

Another accepted theory of those times was that the Dandie resulted from selected specimens of the native rough-haired terrier of the Border country in the Cheviot Hills between England and Scotland. The old Scotch Terrier did not look like the Scottish Terrier of today, but was a longer-bodied, more supple type. This suppleness was developed in the Dandie by careful breedings to make him more adaptable for going to ground in the hunting of everything from rats to badger and fox. Add to this the knowledge we now have of selection for certain characteristics, and this theory is quite believable.

The exhibition of pure-bred dogs at shows in England began in the latter half of the 19th century, and the first classes provided for Dandie Dinmont Terriers were at Manchester in 1861 and in Birmingham in 1862. Some of the early specimens exhibited were thought to be of poor quality and the first place award was withheld. Effort was made to improve stock, and in 1872 a dog owned by Robert and Paul Scott named Peachem was exhibited at the Crystal Palace show and awarded first place. He was described as a good specimen, "not too big, not too little, good in coat, color and top-knot, nicely domed in skull, shapely, well arched in body and not too crooked in front."

The Dandie Dinmont Terrier Club is one of the oldest breed clubs in the British Isles, the Bulldog Club and Bedlington Terrier Club having been established slightly earlier. The first meeting was held on November 17, 1875, and the breed standard was adopted on September 5, 1876. Changes to the breed standard were made in 1877, 1892 and 1901. The original standard served the breed well up until the 1990s, when both the English standard and the American standard were reformatted and updated. Both countries took advantage of their respective kennel club's desire to reformat and added information that might once have been common knowledge to stockmen and farmers in the 19th century, but were mysteries to the modern-dog fanciers of the present, i.e., those not steeped in the basics of animal husbandry, canine anatomy and gait.

The first Dandie Dinmont Terrier Club show was held in 1877 in Carlisle with an entry of 85 Dandies. A 20-pound dog named Shamrock, owned by the Reverend S. Tenison Mosse, won that day, scoring 78 out of a possible 100 points. This was the first time the Dandie had been judged on a scale of points and apparently the last, since the system was not used again. I think it safe to say that today most knowledge-able judges will tell you that it is the overall picture that is important, and one can never evaluate a dog based solely on parts.

The time between 1890 and 1920 saw the emergence of numerous successful breeders of Dandies, and their prefixes can be found in the pedigrees of many of today's Dandies the world over. These names include: Alpin, Ainsty, Bellmead, Darenth, Dogari, Gardenside, Gladsmuir, Hatton, Hendell, Howcaple, Shrimpney, Slitrig, Sowden and two kennels of great longevity, Salismore and Waterbeck.

Mrs. Phyllis Salisbury, whose father

Ch. Salismore May Queen, bred and owned by Mrs. Phyllis Salisbury, England.

Original oil painting by John Emms, circa 1880.

kept Dandies, began exhibiting her Salismore stock in 1922, winning the Dog Challenge Certificate at Crufts with Salismore Sporran, a dog bred by George Jardine, Sr., but it did not carry his Waterbeck prefix. Salismore Dandies have been the foundation stock for many long-time Dandie breeders in the British Isles, as well as abroad. Mrs.

Salisbury's daughter, Audrey Parlby, joined her mother in the breeding and exhibiting of Dandies, and both were approved judges of the breed. Salismore enjoyed great success in the show rings over many decades with such favorites as Eng. Chs. Salismore Mustard, Silversand, Parsley, Watersend Pioneer, Barvae Peppi and Scattercash.

THE INTERNATIONAL CONNECTION

It's interesting to note the influence Salismore has had on Dandies worldwide. Salismore Parsley's influence was felt strongly in America as her daughter, Ch. Salismore Peasblossom (by Bellmead Delphic) was imported to America by Dr. M. Josephine Deubler of Philadelphia, Pennsylvania. Before heading across the pond, Peasblossom was bred to Salismore Proctor, and two of that litter also came to Dr. Deubler. They were Chs. Salismore Peashooter and Playboy. Another imported by Dr. Deubler was

Group of Dandie Dinmont Terriers, owned by W. H. Dunn and A. Mutter. From a painting by John Emms, circa 1879–1890.

Original oil painting on panel by Sir Edwin Landseer, RA, circa 1840.

Ch. Salismore Silversand (by Eng./Am. Ch. Waterbeck Watermark, a litter he sired before he left Britain). All of these imports did important winning in America and made considerable contributions to the fledgling American Dandie.

Waterbeck was another highly successful Dandie kennel of longstanding, getting its start about the same time as Salismore and lasting about as long. Mr. George Jardine, Sr. was its founder, and he was joined in the enterprise by his two sons, John and George, Jr. Watermark was among the most famous Waterbecks. In the early 1950s Watermark amassed 13 Challenge Certificates and sired enough quality offspring before he left for America to win the English Coronation Cup as the breed's top sire three successive years, 1954 through 1956. In 1957 the Coronation Cup was won by his son. Watermark was imported by Miss Sarah Swift for her Cliffield kennels in New York, and he continued his profound influence on the breed. By the end of the century, Watermark had sired 23 American champions, including a top-winning import, Ch. Salismore Silversand, Eng./Am. Ch. Cliffield Larry Langwham, who was exported to the Waterbeck kennels in Scotland, and Ch. Swan Cove Highland Hercules. The influence of Ch. Swan Cove Highland Hercules on the American Dandie was far-reaching, as he was the great-grandsire of the breed's top sire in America, Ch. Woodbourne Knight-Errant, with over 40 champion get. Indeed, when Mr. Jardine, Sr. judged the 1963 Dandie Dinmont Terrier Club of America's national specialty, it was Ch. Swan Cove

Ch. Swan Cove Highland Hercules, one of Watermark's most influential progeny.

Ch. Hendell Pippin, who was retained by her breeder Mrs. Peggy Hulme. Loelia was also Best in Show at the Dandie Dinmont Championship Show at Carlisle under American terrier expert Dr. Deubler. In America, Loelia was put to another British import, Ch. Barvae Percy, and produced one of America's most influential sires, Ch. Kiltie's Choice of Highland, with 24 champion get, including the breed's top-producing sire, Ch. Woodbourne Knight-Errant. To illustrate what a very small world the international Dandie fancy is, note that Barvae Percy was a litter brother of Barvae Peppi, a dog exhibited success-fully by Mrs. Salisbury in England.

A fourth Watermark brother, Ch. Weir of Waterbeck, was imported and owned by Mr. and Mrs. William W. Brainard, Jr., who bred under the Downsbragh prefix. Weir was used at stud and sired a number of champions.

The first Waterbeck export in 1947 to the Cliffield kennels was a bitch named Ch. Flornell Beetham Skittle. She enjoyed the show ring and was the first of her breed to catch the attention of the dog fancy outside the Dandie devotees. Skittles also distinguished herself in the whelping box with eight champion offspring. Skittles and Watermark were related through their dams, Skittles out of Salismore Manuscript, a Bellmead Document daughter, and Watermark out of Winifred of Waterbeck, a Document granddaughter.

Another noteworthy Dandie was sent from America to England in the early 1990s. The pepper dog Ch.

Highland Hercules who won Best of Breed.

Watermark's brother, Ch. Wassail of Waterbeck, also came to Miss Swift, and while he didn't enjoy quite the show-ring success of his brother, he did sire 29 champion offspring. However, none of his get was as influential as the top producers coming down from his brother Watermark.

Another brother, Waterbeck Warrin, would have considerable influence on American Dandies through his daughter, Colislinn Tamara. She was bred to Red Gleam of Hatton and produced the bitch Ch. Hendell Colislinn Loelia, who was exported to the Highland kennels of Mr. and Mrs. Charles Nelson of Utah. Before being exported, Loelia was put to Hendell Bellmead Daring and produced two influential offspring, Ch. Hendell Pocket Prince, who also was later exported to the Nelsons, and a daughter,

Pennywise Postage Due, bred and owned by Catherine B. Nelson of Potomac, Maryland, was imported by David Murray, who added his "at Bencharra" as a suffix to the dog's name when he was registered with The Kennel Club of England. "Benjamin," as he is called, was whelped in 1990, sired by Ch. Dunsandle Postmark, and out of Ch. Pennywise Scarlett O'Hair.

Benjamin has made a significant impact on British Dandies, having been a prolific and influential sire. In fact, it is rather difficult to find a modern British pedigree where Benjamin does not appear in the first or second generation. Benjamin sired 13 English champions, as well as many more with titles overseas. In the show ring he was the top Dandie in England in 1994 but, more importantly, the breed's top champion-producing sire from 1996 through 1999, and the top terrier sire for 1999. His impact has been felt further in that his offspring have been exported to Scandinavia, Western Europe, Australia and New Zealand.

THE DANDIE IN AMERICA

The first Dandies found their way to America from Scotland, and in 1886 three were registered with the American Kennel Club, all owned by Mr. and Mrs. John E. Naylor of Chicago, Illinois. All were peppers, a dog named Bonnie Britton and two bitches, Pride of Leader and Pansy of Leader. The first American champion was a mustard dog named King O' The Heather, imported from England by Edward Brooks of Boston, Massachusetts. The imports did all the

winning in the early days, and it wasn't until 1931 that Auld Pepper O' The Ark (a bitch) and Auld Nick (a dog), bred and owned by Mrs. Lawrence Illoway of Buccleuch kennels, finished their titles.

In 1932 the Dandie Dinmont Terrier Club of America was founded by a small group of fanciers, including Mr. R. Stockton White and his daughter, Mrs. Lawrence (Katherine) Illoway. Katherine Illoway remained an active member, breeder and exhibitor all of her life, well into the latter part of the 20th century, breeding Dandies under the Buccleuch prefix. The first American-bred Dandie group winner was Mrs. Illoway's Ch. Buccleuch Clinker in 1951.

The first Dandie Dinmont Terrier Club of America specialty was held in Greenwich, Connecticut in 1932 with a British import, Ch. Alexander of Clane O'Windholme, winning Best of Breed. World War II intervened and the specialty was not held between 1943 and 1947. The specialty has been held

CREDITED FOR THE SOURCE

The Dandie is credited, by most authorities, as being the source of the wire coat in the Wirehaired variety of the Dachshund. The Wirehaired Dachshunds, until late in the 20th century, had a wider skull, sometimes adorned with silky hair, and a more pronounced arch over their loin than the Smooth and Longhaired Dachshund varieties. The temperament of the Wire variety is also different, being a little more gay, carefree and fun-loving than their more intense brethren.

annually ever since and has moved from being an exclusive East Coast fixture to every other year at Montgomery County Kennel Club, Pennsylvania, and alternate years in another area of the country.

The Early Years in America

Early in the '50s, Miss Carol M. Canora's bitch, Overhill Ramona, bred by Mrs. Helen Kirby (Overhill), was the first Dandie to win an obedience title, her Companion Dog (CD).

The Cliffield kennels of Miss Sarah H. Swift dominated much of the activity in the show rings in the '50s. Her imported bitch Ch. Flornell Beetham Skittle was four times Best of Breed (BOB) at the club's specialty, 1949–1952, and her famous import dog, Eng./Am. Ch. Waterbeck Watermark, won BOB in 1954. A home-bred dog, a Watermark son, Ch. Cliffield Galashiels was BOB in 1959.

Eng./Am. Ch. Waterbeck Watermark, a sire of great influence in the UK and US, and behind most top winners for decades.

Watermark's brother, Ch. Weir of Waterbeck, owned by Mr. and Mrs. William W. Brainard, Jr. was BOB in 1953 and 1955. A son of Ch. Waterbeck Watermark, Am./Eng. Ch. Salismore Silversand, owned by Dr. M. Josephine Deubler's Glespin kennels, won three specialties, 1956–1958, and was usually handled by Jimmy Butler.

American-bred Ch. Glespin B. Brown, a son of Ch. Salismore Silversand and out of Bellmead Scintillate, bred by Dr. M. Josephine Deubler and owned by Mrs. A. E. Johnston, won the 1960 specialty under Mrs. Lawrence Illoway. Mrs. Johnston, an ardent Dandie supporter, nearly five decades later can still be found exhibiting Dandies. Dr. Deubler's import Ch. Salismore Playboy won the specialty in 1961.

The 1962 specialty was held at Westchester Kennel Club in New York, and 24 Dandies were shown to George Jardine of the well-known Waterbeck kennels of Scotland. It was noted that every top win at the specialty went to offspring of Ch. Waterbeck Watermark and son, Ch. Swan Cove Highland Hercules, who was also the BOB winner.

The 1963 specialty returned to Westchester with Heywood R. Hartley judging. BOB went to Seymour N. Weiss's owner-handled mustard bitch, Ch. Ceolaire Bannockburn, a Ch. Swan Cove Highland Hercules daughter.

The 1964 specialty was won by the mustard dog Ch. Laurelane's Dandie Lion, owned by Mr. and Mrs. Hillel S. Levinson under judge Len Carey.

Mrs. Phyllis Salisbury (Salismore) judged the 1965 specialty, awarding Miss Sarah Swift's mustard dog Ch. Cliffield's Cross Keys Colin BOB.

In 1967 Percy Roberts judged an entry of 23 Dandies at the specialty, awarding Charles and Gerri Ross's Ch. Brigadoon Cluanie Coorie BOB, with her son, Ch. Derrick of Ross-Dhu, Best of Opposite Sex. There were two specialties this year; the second one was also won by Ch. Brigadoon Cluanie Coorie.

The judge for the 1968 specialty was Dr. M. Josephine Deubler, and she awarded Mr. and Mrs. John W. Davies, Jr.'s pepper dog, Ch. Woodbourne High Flying Flag, BOB. The following year the import Ch. Barvae Percy won the specialty. He was owned by Miss Florence Newton; he won it again in 1970.

THE 1970S IN AMERICA

The decade began with the introduction of the DDTCA's Code of Ethics, an outline defining the purpose of the club and breeding principles to which all of its members agreed to follow. It is interesting to note that four years later in July 1974, member Ginnie Thorp wrote a scathing piece in the club's quarterly newsletter, *Mustard and Pepper*, about the perceived lack of consideration and apparent total disregard for the Code of Ethics displayed by some of the club's members. It's funny how all of these years later this discussion could easily be raised again, proving how difficult it is to legislate ethical behavior or dictate good manners.

PERSPECTIVE ON MOVEMENT

It was noted by *Popular Dog* columnist Henry A. Bultman that in 1966 there were 27 new American champions and every one was American-bred. It was considered unusual not to have an import or two on the list. Mr. Bultman also writes that, "Movement is becoming a problem in many breeds, and Dandies have had their share of trouble, including disqualifications, at several shows. This can be a highly controversial subject. There are those who say that Dandies are 'naturally' bad movers and their 'normal gait' is easily misinterpreted as lameness. Others will blame temperament—their dog 'could move well if it wanted to but it's being sulky today.'"

He goes on to say, "There does not seem to be any 'standard' that defines correct movement. The breed standard describes a 'model,' and theoretically if the dog is properly constructed, it can perform satisfactorily. Here is one of the many ways a serious breeder can contribute to the progress of a breed. Keep a complete record of each dog's faults, as well as its good points. If 'bad movement' keeps showing up over several generations, we have a fault which probably will be perpetuated unless we use selective breeding." Mr. Bultman's comments could easily be applied to the entries of today just as they were applied almost forty years ago.

June 1970 marked the introduction to the club's members of the first pedigree handbook beginning with the breed's first champion, Ch. King O' The Heather, bred by James Armstrong and owned by Edward Brooks, sired by Charlie II and out of Heather Susie. T. Allen Kirk, Jr., M.D., was the handbook's first chairman, and he wrote an introduction to his work. He writes: "When one enters into the dog game

Ch. Wassail of Waterbeck, whelped 1966 by George Jardine, Scotland, and exported to Miss Sarah H. Swift, sired 29 champions.

Ch. Brigadoon Telstar, whelped 1968 by Robert B. Harrison and owned by Mrs. Doris Oakley.

with the aim of producing a high quality dog or so of any breed, it will take a little time to build a background of knowledge on which to base the breeding program. Much time and a great deal of expense can be saved by this approach.

"When I started breeding Scottish Terriers, I had not learned this. Nine years later, having started over for a fourth time, I won my first blue ribbon. True, an apprenticeship had been served. I know how to lose gracefully. But how much energy loss and disappointment could have been avoided, had I taken the time to think and read?

"When I was introduced to the Dandie Dinmont, a few years back, I became fascinated with him. Soon, fascination gave way to a desire to have a few around, and to produce a few good ones. I took the time to read, and found the standard didn't tell me all I wanted to know, so I went to England and visited some of the kennels of Dandies there, attended the Specialty at Carlisle on two occasions. By then, I felt I knew the breed well enough to start out. By then, too, I had decided what I wanted in a Dandie.

"Having learned the importance of studying a pedigree to work out a proper breeding program, I began to look about for, and compile, pedigrees of the good and of the bad Dandies I saw, in an attempt to trace the sources of the good and bad traits. Finding there was no complete list of Dandie champions available, and having gathered together such a list along with many of the pedigrees of the dogs involved, I felt it would be a worthwhile project to Dandie breeders if a complete chronologic list of these champions were to be published. Happily, the Dandie Club agreed...

"By studying the breeding patterns of the champions of the past, and of the present, perhaps an insight into breeding programs can be obtained so that even better Dandies may be produced in the future. Remember, when you plan to breed 'Little Susie,' the top dog of this year may be a great dog, but the poorest possible stud for her, while a dog only fair himself could be the best. It is not how many

champions appear in your litter's pedigree, but which one, and where."

In that short introduction to one of the most worthy projects the DDTCA ever mounted is advice worth reading by the novice breeder, as well as a reminder to all breeders of long standing.

In 1971 the DDTCA adopted what was called a statement of movement, not included in the official breed standard. It reads: "Proper movement requires a free and easy stride, reaching forward with the front legs and driving with evident force from the rear. The legs move in a straight plane from shoulder to pad (allowing for a turnout of the front feet) and hip to pad, with the pads being placed progressively closer to a center line as the speed increases. A stiff, stilted, hopping or weaving gait and lack of drive in the rear quarters are faults to be penalized."

In April 1975 members of the DDTCA expressed their concern over the adoption of the statement on movement and wished to revisit the matter before the statement was circulated to the judges. Of particular concern was "allowing for a turnout of the front feet" and "with the pads being placed progressively closer to a center line as the speed increases." The matter was put on hold until the club's annual meeting in October that year, and meanwhile such luminaries in the breed as Miss Sarah Swift of Cliffield weighed in, asking the advice of Mrs. Rachel Page Elliott, an internationally recognized expert on the subject of structure and movement. Miss Swift

Ch. Woodbourne Fancy Free, whelped 1968, breeder/owners Mr. and Mrs. John W. Davies, Jr., and handled by John Davies. "Cher," as she was called, was sired by Ch. Barvae Percy out of Ch. Woodbourne Blythe Spirit.

disputed the stated tendency toward single-tracking; she was thinking double-tracking was more correct and wondered what Mrs. Elliott's opinion was on the subject. In a letter dated August 17, 1973, written by Mrs. Elliott to Miss Swift, she writes, "I think much of the problem concerning the term

A famous winner from days gone by, Ch. Barvae Percy, 1970 handled by Peter Green.

A CENTURY LATER...

In January 1975, *Mustard and Pepper* carried a nice piece by Phyllis Salisbury, known worldwide for her Salismore Dandies in England, entitled "Where are we going?". She writes, "A question that may interest breeders is whether the Dandies of today still maintain all the quality and true type that so many fine Dandies have portrayed through the century since the standard was drawn up at Selkirk in 1875. Although the men who drew up this standard, who incidentally bred and worked their Dandies, permitted weights from 10 to 24 pounds, they still considered that 18 pounds was the ideal and that is what we aim for today. It is a well known fact that an outstanding small Dandie is not so often seen as a handsome specimen that exceeds the limit given in the standard.

"One of the main essentials missing today is that look of breeding and quality which is so difficult to define but yet so indispensable and not to be associated with short necks and backs, heavy shoulders and high set tails but rather with lengthy, supple bodies with a gradual rise over the loins. This arch is not to be confused with a roached back where the arch begins just behind the withers. A Dandie with the correct conformation can be readily appreciated when his activity and speed are seen in competition with one of the cobby types. The fact that the hindquarters are very powerful and the legs slightly longer than the forelegs produces the necessary impulsion and activity, both of which are so important in the breed."

Mrs. Salisbury goes on to talk about the terrier mouth and jaw and their obvious importance and then speaks about the breed's two colors. "Mustard and pepper are the only two recognized colors with the crisp outer coat coming through a close undercoat forming what is termed 'pencils.' The throat and jaws are generously protected with stronger hair than the head which is well covered with hair of a very soft silky texture and in the case of a pepper is silvery white in color and in the mustard, creamy white. This makes a perfect setting for the expressive Dandie eyes which have often been described as the loveliest thing in canine lore. Fine quality low set ears carried close to the cheek and covered with soft hair like a mouse's coat are an important asset for a perfect Dandie head. A good coated specimen does not require drastic stripping and with a little foresight can be shown all the year round.

"The breed today needs some more enthusiastic up and coming young breeders who are willing to appraise and in some cases even discard from their breeding program their own Dandies. Since the days of Tinker Allen these dour little Scottish borderers have given their loyalty and devotion to man so surely we owe it to them to give as much in return."

These are some heady thoughts and are as true today as they were in the 1970s. I wonder how many current breeders could accept Mrs. Salisbury's sage advice to discard their stock if it is not typical or in the best interests of the future of this marvelous little breed?

'double' or 'parallel' tracking systems, as you said, stems from semantics. These expressions are often interpreted to mean parallel perpendicular action rather than the distance between the line of foot prints. Parallel, perpendicular leg movement causes stiltedness and wobbling and reduces reach and drive. Too often, I think, wobbling is mistaken for the slight natural roll that comes from correct build and movement in wide-bodied, short-legged varieties–– such as the Dandie—where at each step of the trot the diagonal thrust is more on a bias to the line of travel than in narrower longer legged types.

"It goes without saying that body structure dictates the degree to which a dog can get his pads and body support under his center of gravity so that the push will be where it counts the most. Nature works consistently in this interest, and the dog that leaves footprints on either side of the line of travel (double or parallel tracking) may be moving just as correctly for his breed as the dog that actually sets his feet more or less on a straight line. But this does not mean he is moving with his legs parallel to each other and perpendicular to the ground. In my opinion any dog is a faulty mover that does not attempt to get his legs near or on the center line of body balance. (Barring, of course, crooked joints or looseness that

causes toeing in, weaving or crossing!)

"I can readily understand your concern about any threat to good Dandie type which could occur by breeding away from the characteristic wide rib spring and deep brisket, as this is part of his unique quality. I must say that I liked the definition of gait which I ran across in a *Popular Dogs* Dandie breed

Ch. Clyde of Ross-Dhu, winning a group in 1973.

Ch. Ceolaire Checkmate, breeder/owner-handled by Carol M. Canora, winning BOB at Devon in 1973 under judge Mrs. Lawrence Illoway.

Ch. Nebshire's Drum Hill Finale, a popular winner from the late 1970s, bred by Mary Nelson Stephenson.

Ch. Overhill Brett, pictured in 1977 with breeder/owner Mrs. William M. Kirby under judge Mary Nelson Stephenson. Brett was a grandson of Ch. Wassail of Waterbeck. Mrs. Kirby was an active breeder in Kansas City through the '60s and '70s who did much to spread the word about the breed.

column a year or two ago (and which I believe has been endorsed by the breed club?) as the writer describes clearly how good drive is accomplished. Fanciers should not interpret this as a statement of single tracking, however. The Dandie is a little dog with a broad base of support (and a long keel!). But like any other breed, he has to reach for that center line of balance in order to travel efficiently. I have an idea that if I could see his trail along a firm wet beach there would be a double line of footprints, even though they might be pretty close together."

Finally, Dr. M. Josephine Deubler, then club secretary, wrote, "The reasons the statement on movement is considered necessary was stated in a club letter from July, 1971, which was sent to all judges licensed to pass on our breed." She goes on to state, "Although this

statement on movement has not been added to our breed standard, it is hoped that we are providing the criteria for both the breeder and judge by which an evaluation can be made as to the proper movement that a Dandie should have. We will sincerely appreciate your efforts, through your judging, to assist us in encouraging breeders and exhibitors of Dandie Dinmont Terriers to continuously strive to improve the movement of Dandies, by breeding and conditioning, so that ultimately an increasing percentage of those Dandies which are shown will adhere to the above statement on movement."

On September 6, 1976, the Dandie national specialty was held off the Eastern Seaboard for the first time, being held in conjunction with the Louisville

on the East Coast, and this time it was at the Heart of America Kennel Club show in Kansas City, Missouri. Two northern California gentlemen, who were great friends, judged: Al Horning (Kilties), a DDTCA member since 1960, judged the sweepstakes and Nick Calicura the regular classes. In a field of 22 sweepstakes youngsters, Best in Sweepstakes went to Tamtop Mercedes of Dancaway, bred by Joan M. McElligott and Gail B. Isner and owned by John and Wendy Brant. She was sired by Ch. Dancaway's Rolls R. MacTweed out of Ch. Tamtop Tassie. In Mr. Horning's critique he commented,

Ch. Dancaway's Bentley MacTweed, UD, whelped in 1975, breeder/owner-handled by Mrs. John R. Brant, Jr., sired ten champions.

Kennel Club show in Kentucky instead. Club member Joanne Rex Cummins judged 24 sweepstakes youngsters, awarding Best in Sweepstakes to a young pepper dog from the Six to Nine Months Class, Charlieshope Tom Terrific, breeder/owner-handled by Carole Neuhardt. Tom was sired by Ch. Nebshire's Dapper Dan out of Ch. Brigadoon Stardust. Dapper Dan sired 17 champions, and Stardust produced 6 champions.

Club member Dr. Lee Huggins judged an entry of 57 dogs in the regular classes at Louisville. BOB went to the mustard dog Ch. Woodbourne Next In Line, bred by John and Nancy Davies, owned by Allan M. Sheimo and Dr. Basilio S. Bolumen and handled by Robert Hutton. "Clark," as he was called, was sired by Graymorn's Mannering out of the top-producing bitch of all time, Ch. Woodbourne Blythe Spirit, dam of 11 champions.

The year 1978 marked the second time the national specialty was not held

With ten all-breed Best in Show wins, Ch. Woodbourne Next In Line, better known as "Clark," set a record for the Dandie Dinmont that stood from 1977 to 2006.

Ch. Woodbourne Knight-Errant, whelped in 1971, bred and owned by Mr. and Mrs. James W. Davies, Jr., became the breed's top sire with 43 champions.

"The presentation of most dogs was pleasing and I believe a good deal of credit for this should be given to the excellent grooming instructions made available by our club. There is one thing I cannot understand. Why would someone spend hours grooming a coat with their fingers and then use clippers on ears and rear ends?"

Under Mr. Calicura this same bitch was Winners Bitch. Mr. Calicura, in an entry of 49, chose the 1976 DDTCA Best

Winner of two national specialties, Ch. Barvae Percy proved an excellent sire as well.

in Sweepstakes winner, Ch. Charlieshope Tom Terrific, as his BOB. Not only was Tom a specialty winner, but he was also a successful sire with 21 champion get. That is not a surprise considering from where he came; quality begets quality.

October 1978 saw the first Certificate of Gameness awarded to a Dandie Dinmont Terrier by the American Working Terrier Association, the precursor to the American Kennel Club earthdog trials that are popular today. That Dandie was Can. Ch. Torcroft Young Bess, bred by Lorna Rindal, sired by Eng./Am. Ch. Hendell Pocket Prince and out of Am./Can. Ch. Torcroft Fiona, owned by Roy and Betty-Anne Stenmark.

Imported from England, Ch. Barvae Percy won the national specialty twice, in 1969 and 1970, and was the sire of the top-producing Ch. Kilties Choice of Highland, a pepper dog who was called "Jiggs," who in turn produced 24 champions. Jiggs in turn sired Ch. Woodbourne Knight-Errant, the breed's top producer of all time with 43 champion get. Top-winning Ch. Clyde of Ross-Dhu won the national specialty four times, 1971, 1972, 1973 and 1975, and he was also the sire of 13 champions. Another top winner of the times, Ch. Nebshire's Drum Hill Finale, bred by Mary Nelson Stephenson and shown by Robert Crews for owner Robert Renn, was the DDTCA national specialty breed winner in 1977. Sired by Ch. Nebshire's Minute Man and out of Gayleward Honi of Drum Hill, he was also BOB at the Westminster Kennel

Club dog show three times and Group second under judge Mrs. Ann Stevenson. The 1979 DDTCA Breed winner, under club member Jeannine Dowell, was a Canadian-bred mustard dog, Ch. Ottersmile Mister MacGerrity; while bred by Robert and Roberta Gibson, he was all owner Joan MacKinnon's Graymorn breeding.

THE 1980s IN AMERICA

A record entry of 62 dogs turned out for the 1981 DDTCA national specialty in the club's 49th year. Puppy sweepstakes was judged by Miss Margaret Davidson (Inzievar) of Scotland. From 22 entries, she chose Glengavin Grey Gwyneth, a bitch bred and owned by Bill and Doris Breuler. Mr. R. Stephen Shaw judged the regular classes and selected Ch. Dancaway's Farley Mowat as BOB. He was handled by his breeder/owner, Mrs. Wendy Brant. Also in 1981, there was the first mention of the decline in numbers of Dandies being bred. At that time the Dandie was regularly in the Top 100 in numbers registered with the AKC, with approximately 200 puppies born annually.

The 50th anniversary of the DDTCA came in 1982. The national specialty was held in Kansas City, Missouri that year with visitors coming from all over the world to celebrate. It was the first year I was president of the DDTCA, and I was very proud to have the honor. Two long-time club members were selected to judge: Mrs. John Neblett (Nebshires) judged 21 sweepstakes youngsters, and one of the breed's most stalwart supporters, Dr. M. Josephine Deubler

(Glespin), judged 63 dogs in the regular classes. Mrs. Neblett selected the young pepper dog Charlieshope Habitforming for Best in Sweepstakes. "Kip," as he was called, was bred by Carole W. Neuhardt and owned by Catherine B. Nelson. Dr. Deubler's choice for BOB was the pepper veteran bitch Ch. Shadowmark's Martini Time, bred by Rita Lawson, owned by Dr. Tom Greene and handled by Peter Green. This specialty saw the debut of the new club pin and a handsome pewter Dandie statue by club member and artist Patsy Davis. This statue has since been awarded to subsequent Best in Sweepstakes winners.

Dr. Deubler's critique from the specialty was interesting. She writes in the club's newsletter, "My general impression is that the breed still lacks uniformity—we see too few Dandies which are long, strong and flexible, with the correct topline. Size continues to be a problem, with overweight a

Ch. Nebshire's Drum Hill Finale, handled by Robert Crews, was Best of Breed at the 1977 national specialty under judge Anne Rogers Clark.

TOP: Ch. Charlieshope Tom Terrific, whelped January 1976, at seven months of age, bred/owned/handled by Carole Neuhardt under judge Mrs. Joanne Rex Cummings (Durbin). BOTTOM: Ch. Charlieshope Tom Terrific, all grown up now at three-and-a-half years of age under judge Barbara Fournier.

contributing factor. Trimming has improved over the years but there is still a tendency to exaggerate. The standard calls for a thin feather on the ear coming to a distinct point. I felt that head covering and furnishings were over-done in some cases. The correct double coat, which requires months of grooming and trimming, was lacking in a number of the Dandies; either coats were soft and single or there was a fairly hard coat with little or no undercoat. There were some with long muzzles and narrow skulls and a few with short forefaces—both not the 3 to 5 muzzle to skull proportions called for by the standard.

"The major problem, in my opinion, was bites. The correct scissors bite was the exception rather than the rule. The most recent change in the standard eliminated the word 'level' which had been interpreted as referring to a pincers bite (upper and lower incisors meeting tip to tip) rather than to evenly spaced incisors. The only correct bite is a tight scissors bite with the upper incisors overlapping the lower. Undershot, overshot and pincer bites should be avoided."

The 1983 national specialty was back at Montgomery County Kennel Club with Nancy Mann (Woodbourne) passing on 19 sweepstakes entries, finding her Best in Sweepstakes in Rorralore Au Contraire—bred, owned and shown by Charlotte Clem McGowan. Mrs. Ann Stevenson had 59 dogs in the regular classes, finding Ch. Muldoon's Druid of Montizard for BOB. "Drim," as he was called, had been Best of Opposite Sex twice at prior national specialties, so it was nice to see this dog finally prevail. He was bred by his co-owner, Mrs. Sugie Larsen, and co-owned and handled by Doug Young.

In 1984 the national specialty went to northern California with an entry of 16 sweepstakes youngsters for Mrs. Carole Neuhardt (Charlieshope) to judge. Her winner was Wincidell Charcoal Chastity who was bred, owned and handled by Hank Kauffman. Chastity was sired by Ch. Charlieshope Habitforming out of Ch. Durbin Honesty of Wincidell. Mrs. Lydia Coleman Hutchinson passed on 53 in the regular classes, finding the mustard bitch Ch.

Charlieshope Au Courant, bred by Carole Neuhardt and owned and handled by Charlotte Clem McGowan, for BOB. "Cricket," as she was called, had been Best of Opposite Sex at several previous specialties.

In Belmont, California in 1984, the first fruitful meeting took place of the group who would work for more than 12 long years putting the club's illustrated standard together. Club members with artistic abilities, Dr. Tom Greene, Richard Yoho and Cathy Nelson, worked on the drawings, and much to the board's amazement there was uniform agreement on what constituted a correct Dandie! Who would have thought that possible? The committee consisted of all of the DDTCA officers and directors. That year also saw a continuing decline in the popularity of the Dandie, with only 162 puppies registered that year, and the breed ranked 110th out of 128 AKC-recognized breeds.

The 1985 specialty was back at Montgomery County Kennel Club with Mrs. Karen Dorn (Derrydown) judging 15 sweepstakes youngsters, awarding Best of Sweepstakes to Pennywise Scarlett O'Hair, bred and owned by Cathy Nelson and handled by her husband John. Mr. Seymour Weiss (Montrose) judged 52 in the regular classes, awarding BOB to Ch. Pennywise Calamity Jamie, bred and owned by Cathy Nelson and co-owned by Diane Taliaferro.

Gaithersburg, Maryland was the site of the 1986 national specialty. Mrs. Catherine B. Nelson (Pennywise) judged

an entry of 13, awarding Best in Sweepstakes to King's Mtn. Stardust, bred and owned by Roy and Betty-Anne Stenmark and co-owned by Vern and Anne Wilson. Mrs. Mike Macbeth Goodfellow (Glahms) judged 43 in the regular classes, awarding BOB to Ch. Sandkastle Kosciusko Bridge, who was bred by Michael and Diana Helfner, owned by Emily Holden and K. Carol Carlson and handled by Elliott Weiss. In 1986 the Dandie registered only 130 Dandies with the AKC and its ranking dropped to 114th.

The 1987 national specialty returned to Montgomery County Kennel club with Mrs. Linda Bergh (Horizons) judging 19 sweepstakes youngsters, awarding Best in Sweepstakes to Pennywise Butterfly McQueen, breeder/owner/handler Cathy Nelson. Miss Felicity E. Soutter (Drevaburn) judged a record entry of 73 in the regular classes, awarding BOB to the class bitch, Abington's Wingate's Fancy, bred by Phillip and Lois Hayman and owned by Lois Weiner.

Winning the Breed under judge Robert Graham, Ch. Sandkastle Kosciusko Bridge, handled by a very young and dashing Elliott B. Weiss, bred by Diana K. and Michael L. Helfner and owned by K. Carol Carlson and Emily Holden.

Ch. Shadowmark's Martini Time, pepper bitch, whelped in 1975, bred by Jack Ball and Rita Lawson, owned by Thomas E. Greene, M.D., handled by Peter Green. Shown winning BOB in 1978 at Montgomery County Kennel Club.

In 1987 the AKC announced a program for improving the breed standards and published the following statement: "We want to emphasize we are not recommending changing standards. However, we will be evaluating your standard and where we think greater clarity is required, whether it is because of missing description, incomplete or insufficient description, incorrect or ambiguous terminology or poor sentence construction, such shortcomings will be cited."

In 1987 the AKC desired that all parent clubs bring their standard into conformity with a new recommended format for standard order and content. Standardized terminology was to be used in all standards. The AKC published a "Guide for Writing Breed Standards" with the format for standard order and content. They urged the use of Harold R. Spira's *Canine Terminology* as the reference source for standardizing terminology. If you're not familiar with Dr. Spira's wonderful book, it is the canine version of *Webster's English Dictionary* and a must in any serious dog fancier's library. John J. Mandeville, then Director of the AKC Judging Research & Development Department, reviewed the existing Dandie standard and wrote, "The present Dandie standard can probably be best character-ized as surprisingly good for one that's missing so much."

The DDTCA seized this opportu-nity to fill in the blanks on the woefully inadequate Dandie breed standard. Missing was a "General Appearance" descrip-tion, mention of substance, eye rim pigmentation, a stop, planes of the skull and muzzle, nose,

Ch. Woodbourne Next In Line, whelped 1973, bred by Mr. and Mrs. John W. Davies, Jr., owned by Allan M. Sheimo and Dr. Basilio Bolumen, winning the 1976 specialty, handled by Robert Hutton. Judge is Dr. Lee Huggins, and the trophy presenter Mrs. Carole Neuhardt, President of the DDTCA in 1976.

lips and flews, underline, tuck-up, croup, forequarter angulation, shoulders and shoulder blades, point of shoulder, upper arm, elbows, pasterns, rear angulation, upper thighs, stifles, second thighs, hock joints, hocks and any mention of toes and/or pads of the feet. A long list indeed. I chaired the committee and worked along with Dr. Josephine Deubler, Gail Isner, Cathy Nelson, Seymour Weiss and Richard Yoho. There was very little disagreement among the DDTCA membership over these inclusions in the breed standard, and I think that was in part because the same standardizing was going on in England, and we were remarkably similar in our descriptions.

In 1988 the specialty was back in northern California, with an entry of 21 in the sweepstakes for Mrs. Gail Isner (Tamtop). Her winner was Derrydown Jercat Rockafella, bred by Karen Dorn, owned by Cathie and Jerry Spencer and handled by Christie Maxfield. Mrs. Jeannine Dowell judged 55 in the regular classes and awarded BOB to Ch. Munchkintown Baxter of Kemp, bred by Nanette E. Armstrong, owned by Thomas Lewisky and Edward Murray and handled by Wood Wornall.

In the early 1980s, the AKC began producing slide shows for every AKC-recognized breed. By the time they got to the Dandie, videos were the norm and slide shows a thing of the past. The same committee which continued to work on the illustrated standard, as well as the standardizing of the breed standard, was appointed to work with the AKC to produce a video acceptable by all involved. Terrier judge Mrs. Phyllis Haage was the judge consultant appointed by the AKC to work with the DDTCA's committee and this relationship proved a good one for all concerned. All these years later I can say that I like most of what I see on that video we filmed on October 4, 1989.

September 20, 1989 marked the day club member Velma Longhorn died in a car accident near her home. Velma and her partner Dora Ortwein owned the Kamlo Dandies located in Sonoma, California. The loss of Velma to the ever-dwindling pool of devoted Dandie breeders was deeply felt. The filming of the AKC Dandie breed video was scheduled a few weeks after this tragic event and one of the Kamlo Dandies was featured prominently in this video.

My husband Roy judged the 1989 specialty at Montgomery with an entry of 52 and put to BOB a pepper dog, Ch. Dunsandle Postmark, bred by France Roozen, owned by Barbara and James

Ch. Kamlo's Ginger Spice, with breeder/owner Velma Longhorn, under judge Peter B. Thomson.

Ch. Charlieshope Au Courant, whelped in 1979, bred by Carole W. Neuhardt, owned and shown by Charlotte Clem McGowen. "Cricket" was sired by Ch. Charlieshope Tom Terrific out of Ch. Charlieshope Sassy Sara.

Monroe and handled by Donna Johnston. Club president Richard Yoho awarded Best in Sweepstakes to Winsan Kelley's Solitaire out of a field of 12, co-bred by Mary Neely-Scott and owners Sandra and Winston Stuart.

THE 1990S IN AMERICA
The 1990 specialty was also held at Montgomery, since the club had voted to support the 25th anniversary of the Great Western Terrier Association in southern California by holding the 1991

Ch. Muldoon's Druid of Montizard, winning Best of Breed at Montgomery County Kennel Club 1983 under Ann Stevenson.

specialty there. Mrs. Mary Neely-Scott judged the sweepstakes and was honored with an entry of 23 youngsters, putting to Best in Sweepstakes Peggy Carr's home-bred pepper bitch Schooners Bunny Run. Mr. Robert Graham judged 61 in the regular classes, selecting Ch. Dunsandle Postmark as BOB, a repeat of his 1989 win.

The Dandie specialty in 1991 went to the Great Western Terrier Association in Pasadena, California. Steven Houser, partner of club President Richard Yoho, judged 23 sweepstakes entries. His winner was Derrydown Johnny Be Good, bred and owned by Karen Dorn and Myron Stahl. Robert Moore judged 63 in the regular classes, putting to BOB Ch. Derrydown Heartlight—bred by Karen Dorn, owned by Karen and Carol Ann Stahl and handled by Geoff Browne.

The AKC statistics for registrations showed that once again the Dandie had dropped in numerical standings to 124th out of 134 AKC-recognized breeds.

The specialty was back at Montgomery in 1992, with Mrs. Anita Kay Simpson judging ten sweepstakes youngsters selecting a personal favorite of mine, the mustard bitch Pennywise Brier Patch, as Best in Sweepstakes. Brier Patch was bred by Cathy Nelson and owned by Ed and Gail Isner. Mrs. Peggy Hulme (Hendell) judged 37 in the regular classes and gave BOB to Ch. Pennywise The Butler Did It, making for a spectacular year for his breeder/owner/handler Cathy Nelson. The year was the 60th anniversary of the club.

February 1993 marked a first for the Dandie when breeder/owner/handler Cathy Nelson piloted her mustard dog Ch. Pennywise The Butler Did It to first in the group at the Westminster Kennel Club dog show under judge Ruth Cooper. Butler had placed third in the group at Westminster the previous year under judge Michelle Billings. It was a great win for Cathy and Butler and also a great win for the breed as members of the general public were intrigued with this dog, and many puppy inquiries to breeders all over the country followed.

The 1994 specialty at Montgomery saw Mrs. Karen Dorn judging 17 sweepstakes youngsters awarding Best in Sweepstakes to Pennywise Gambit—bred, owned and handled by Catherine B. Nelson. Mr. Kenneth A. McDermott judged 46 in the regular classes. BOB went to Ch. Pennywise Brier Patch, the sweepstakes winner from 1992.

Northern California was once again the site of the specialty in 1995, with Ms. Norma Ryan judging eight sweepstakes entries, putting to Best in Sweepstakes MacKilty's Scot Ham-L-Ton, bred and owned by Nancy Herman. Dr. Samuel Draper judged 43 in the regular classes, putting to BOB the mustard dog Ch. Pennywise King's Mtn. MVP, bred by Catherine Nelson and owned by Max and Linda Spurlock.

In July 1995 the club's *Handbook of Champions* was published in the new format, a large three-ring binder with photographs accompanying the information and pedigree on each new champion. Thanks go to Gail Isner for data input and Cathy Nelson for photos

and production for this enormous and helpful work. Updates are published every few years, and the handbook has become invaluable to Dandie breeders.

In 1996 the specialty was back at Montgomery, with Mrs. Joan B. MacKinnon from Canada judging the ten sweepstakes youngsters, putting to Best in Sweepstakes Keleigh Dixieland Brass, bred and owned by Linda Messer.

Ch. Charlieshope Habitforming, bred by Carole Neuhardt and owned by Cathy Nelson, winning under judge Seymour Weiss.

Ch. Pennywise The Butler Did It, winning the group under judge Mrs. Ruth Cooper at the 1993 Westminster Kennel Club Show with handler Cathy Nelson.

Ch. Dunsandle Postmark, whelped in 1987, bred by France Roozen and owned by Barbara and James B. Monroe, winning the 1989 specialty under Roy Stenmark.

Mrs. Phyllis Hamilton Haage judged 37 in the regular classes, putting the veteran dog Ch. Pennywise The Butler

The late Mary Neely-Scott with her Elfkin Solitaire.

Did It to BOB— bred, owned and handled by Catherine Nelson.

The specialty went to Colorado Springs in 1997 with Mrs. Catherine B. Nelson judging nine sweepstakes youngsters and awarding Best in Sweepstakes to King's Mtn. Pixie Montizard, bred and owned by Betty-Anne Stenmark and Doug Young. Dr. Harry Smith judged 37 in the regular classes, awarding BOB to Ch. Glengarry Chatterbox, bred by Linda Winfrey and owned by Karen (also the handler) and Phil Cramer. Ch. Kamlo's Raise'N A Rumpus earned her Utility level title in three obedience trials in a row. Rumpus is owned, trained and shown by Lee Palmer, who has shown many Dandies to their obedience titles, proving it can be done.

In 1998 Dr. Merlyn Green judged 15 sweepstakes entries and awarded Best in Sweepstakes to Montizard's Louella Parsons, bred and owned by Doug and Julie Young. Mr. Walter F. Goodman judged 37 in the regular classes, awarding BOB to two-time BOS winner Ch. Pennywise Gambit, bred, owned and handled by Catherine B. Nelson.

Columbus, Ohio was the site of the 1999 specialty, with Mrs. Caroline Darracott (Brucebairn) judging 17 sweepstakes youngsters, putting to Best in Sweepstakes Montizard Backfield'N Motion, bred and owned by Doug and Julie Young. Mrs. James Edward Clark judged 41 in the regular classes. Ch. Glengarry Chatterbox, bred by Linda Winfrey and owned by Phil and Karen Cramer, repeated her 1997 win.

DANDIES IN THE 21ST CENTURY

In the year 2000 Mrs. Linda Bergh (Horizons) from Canada judged the 16 sweepstakes youngsters, awarding Dreamboat Top Of The Class Best in Sweepstakes, bred by Laura Chapal and owned by Karen and Phil Cramer. Mr. Edd E. Bivin judged 38 in the regular classes, awarding BOB to Ch. Glengarry Harley Low Rider, bred and owned by Linda Winfrey, handled by Ernesto Lara.

The Pacific Northwest hosted its first specialty in 2001, with Ms. Christine Maxfield judging 14 sweepstakes entries, awarding Winterways The Albert Best in Sweepstakes, bred by Marja and Nina Talvitie of Finland and owned and handled by Anne Johnston. Mrs. Jeannine M. Dowell judged 39 in the regular classes, awarding BOB to Ch. Tamtop Trooping The Colours, bred and owned by R. Edward and Gail B. Isner and Catherine B. Nelson.

The first AKC/Eukanuba American Dog Classic Invitational was held in Orlando, Florida on December 12, 2001. Mr. Stephen Shaw judged, awarding BOB to Ch. Glengarry Harley Low Rider.

Winning under judge Sandra Goose Allen, Ch. Glengarry Harley Low Rider, bred, owned and handled by Linda Winfrey.

Harley repeated his win in 2002 under judge Mr. Jon Cole.

The 2002 sweepstakes was judged by Miss France Roozen, awarding the Canadian-bred mustard dog bred and owned by Mike Macbeth, Glahms Golden Legacy. Ms. Charlotte Clem McGowan judged the regular classes and put to BOB Cathy Nelson's Ch. Pennywise Hairry Potter.

Ch. Glengarry Chatterbox, winning under judge Dorothy Macdonald, owner-handled by Phil and Karen Cramer, Pastime Dandies.

REVERSING THE TREND: DECLINING NUMBERS

The year 1997 marked the first formal acknowledgment by the club of the breed's biggest problem, declining numbers of puppies bred in this country, and the Board established a "reverse the trend" task force with Jody Moxham heading up the committee to investigate the cause. The committee is still in existence with, unfortunately, little headway having been made in reversing the trend. I believe the problem to be a complex, multi-faceted one with no easy solutions. Even more shocking is the fact that quite a number of the annual registrations are made by so-called puppy-mill breeders. Clearly the breed is in trouble.

Unfortunately there are very few real breeders left in the breed, as opposed to well-intentioned pet owners who breed the bitch they happen to own whether she is really worthy of being bred or not. Today, just because a dog becomes a champion does not necessarily indicate its true worth as breeding stock. Real brood bitches are also the best show bitches. A good brood bitch conceives and free whelps a good-sized litter, at least four puppies and often five or six. These puppies are vigorous and are raised by the bitch without a great deal of help from the breeder, who just keeps a watchful eye on the dam and her brood. Bitches who have difficulty conceiving, who must whelp via Caesarean section, whose puppies are small in size and whose litters consist of only one or two puppies, with perhaps only one surviving, will not help reverse the trend. And if that single surviving puppy is a bitch and is also bred from, in all likelihood she will perpetuate her own dam's problems and may or may not produce a litter at all. These ideas are nothing new and represent what all knowledgeable and successful breeders know.

There are those who believe that because of the small numbers of Dandies being bred that all bitches should be bred, regardless of their quality. I disagree. To breed from dogs who are not of good type and who are not mentally and structurally sound will do nothing to regain the breed's popularity.

Selection of stud dogs must be made with knowledge of the family he comes from, not just the dog himself, and this dog must complement the bitch being bred. Well-bred stud dogs who are stallions will, in all likelihood, reproduce those qualities they have. It is seldom that a bitchy dog will produce better than himself, although it can and does happen. Choosing the stud dog has nothing at all to do with whether he is the current top winner.

The dwindling numbers of Dandies born in this country each year have made many breeders even more cautious about where their breeding stock goes. Unfortunately, despite good intentions, many inquiries are met with less than a receptive attitude by that breeder, leery that his puppy might end up in the hands of an unscrupulous or commercial breeder. Unfortunately the inquirer who is sincere in his interest in the Dandie, who is met with a hostile and less-than-welcoming attitude, will probably move on to a different breed.

Many breeders believe every puppy in their litter is show quality and insist that each puppy be shown to its championship, which is discouraging to people who simply want to enjoy a charming Dandie as their house pet. It is a rare litter indeed where there is more than one or two truly honest show prospects.

Once in a while a new person comes along who is looking to become a serious breeder and wishes to buy the best bitch possible to become the foundation of his breeding program. Sometimes this person is not as serious as hoped and falls by the wayside, as there is no instant gratification in the breeding of good dogs. Often beginning breedings are simply the gathering of all the right parts and the fascination of breeding better dogs is trying to hang all those virtues on the same dog. Breedings are often two steps forward and one back before real progress is realized. One has to remember that sometimes this person becomes a serious member of the Dandie fancy who will help reverse the trend. Serious inquiries need to be met with an open and welcoming attitude. It is best to establish a relationship with this person before selling a quality show and breeding puppy to him. In this way, hopefully, the good puppies fall into the hands of good people who also will be good stewards of the breed.

We must also realize that serious novices must be entrusted with a truly quality puppy so they may meet with some success. If the breeder always keeps the best for himself, then this novice who seldom enjoys a win is likely to become discouraged and drift away from the breed. I believe if this novice is to be entrusted with a puppy at all, he should be entrusted with a good one.

The Dandie has become one of the toughest breeds to groom at a level high enough to be truly competitive. Some people have a natural affinity for the craft and an eye able to truly see the detail. Others will remain workmanlike all of their lives, as real show grooming is an art. New Dandie exhibitors must seek out a knowledgeable and experienced mentor. As in most things in life worth pursuing, it'll take years of listening and learning and paying your dues before you eventually succeed, but it will be most gratifying.

Ch. Pastime Rex Hairison, winning Group 4 under the author at the 2005 AKC/Eukanuba Invitational. Breeders/owners Phil and Karen Cramer.

In 2003, the specialty moved to Knoxville, Tennessee, with Mr. Richard Yoho (Windsedge) judging ten sweepstakes youngsters, awarding Best in Sweepstakes to King's Mtn. Cordelia, bred by Roy and Betty-Anne Stenmark and Sandra Pretari and owned by handler Miriam Couto, Barbara Binder and Betty-Anne Stenmark. Mr. Jon Cole judged 39 in the regular classes, awarding the veteran bitch Ch. Pennywise Gambit BOB, this being her second national victory.

The 2004 specialty was once again back at Montgomery, with Mrs. Marcia Musson (His Nibs) judging ten sweepstakes entries and awarding Best in Sweepstakes to King's Mtn. Stuart Little, breeders/owners Sandra Pretari and Betty-Anne Stenmark. Mr. Elliott Weiss judged 36 in the regular classes, awarding BOB to Ch. Pennywise Hairris Tweed, breeder/owner/handler Catherine B. Nelson.

January 2005 was the fourth edition of the AKC/Eukanuba Invitational in Tampa, Florida, with Mr. W. Ronald Irving, President of The Kennel Club (England), judging nine Dandies and awarding BOB to Ch. Pastime Rex Hairison, bred and owned by Phil and Karen Cramer, and onto a Group 4 under the author.

DANDIES IN AUSTRALIA

Dandies were first seen in Australia in the 1880s and 1890s but had all but disappeared when, in 1970, Mary McCaul imported two Dandies, a dog and a bitch, from Peggy Hulme (Hendell) and the Bellmead kennels.

The dog's name was Eng. Ch. Bellmead Craigvar Callboy. The first Dandie to come was a male but because of a rabies scare in England a bitch didn't arrive for two years. Once Mary had the two she began exhibiting them, and by 1980 there were others interested in the breed and actively showing too. Ms. McCaul wasn't always successful in the show ring, as many judges refused to award the Challenge Certificate because the dogs didn't have level toplines.

In the early 1980s the mustard dog Aust. Ch. Kelty Kavalier was very successful, winning seven all-breed Bests in Show, one of which was under the Canadian breeder and judge Miss Mike Macbeth. He was bred by a Mrs. Lidgett of Bachus Marsh and owned by various people throughout his life, including Adrian and Lee Walmsley (now Mrs. Lee Pieterse).

Unfortunately by 1990 enthusiasm had once again waned, leaving just three breeders of note still active. They were Kathy Crossman (Dandieglen) of South Australia, Gina Tissington (Jimetta) of New South Wales and David and Margaret Harrison (Dandiedale) of Victoria.

In the period between 1986 and 1993, Dr. Emma Greenway and her partner Heather Grudgfield of Victoria were actively breeding and showing Miniature Schnauzers with little success. Their interest turned to the Dandie and after a worldwide search they acquired a pepper bitch from Mrs. Wendy Weatherstone (Borderstone) of England, who generously gave up the only bitch in the litter, a puppy who

Pictured at nine years of age, Eng. Ch. Borderstone Black-N-Blue, bred and owned by Wendy Weatherstone.

would become the foundation bitch at Jollygaze. She was Aust. Ch. Borderstone Dawn Dancer, called "Betsy," a bitch who was long, shapely and sound-moving. She was by Eng./Am. Ch. Pennywise Postage Due at Bencharra out of Eng. Ch. Borderstone Black-N-Blue. Betsy won her Australian champi-onship, and her show record included an all-breeds Best in Show. More importantly she proved her worth in the

Aust./N.Z. Ch. Jollygaze Arising Sun, better known as "Gordon."

whelping box as well. At this time Jollygaze also acquired Aust. Ch. Dandiedale Rupert Bear or "Paddy," a dog of all Australian breeding.

In 1995 Betsy was bred to Paddy, a mating which produced the mustard dog Aust./N.Z. Ch. Jollygaze Arising Sun, called "Gordon." Gordon won the group at the 1997 Sporting Terrier Club of Victoria, in a field of more than 500 terriers under Mr. Ronnie Irving, currently Chairman of The Kennel Club (England) and himself a Dandie owner.

Betsy was also put to Paddy's sire, Aust. Ch. Jimetta M Bas Strait, and produced a litter of five puppies, three of which went on to become Australian champions and two of those were all-breed Best in Show winners. Two would also go on to have a profound influence on the breed worldwide: Aust./N.Z. Ch. Jollygaze Baltizar Dawn, known as "Edward," a two-time all-breed Best in Show winner, and his sister, Jollygaze Bonny Bluebell.

Edward has been a prolific sire both at home and abroad. He was put to N.Z. Ch. Hobergays Besom (by Eng. Ch. Renald Ulysses out of N.Z. Ch. Betic Dulcamara) to produce Hobergays Drummer Boy, called "Macbeth," and Hobergays Dream Dancer. Macbeth grew to be too large but his breed type, including a wonderfully long and curvy body and big angles fore and aft, have proved valuable to the gene pool. Edward was also put to Aust. Ch. Hobergays Gussie Gumdrop (by Aust./N.Z. Ch. Jollygaze Golly Gosh out of N.Z. Ch. Hobergays Besom) and produced Aust. Ch. Jollygaze Quick

Step or "Quibble," who is now in California at King's Mtn., as well as Jollygaze Quintessential, who resides in British Columbia, Canada with Janice Mullins.

Bonny Bluebell was put to imported frozen semen from Can. Ch. Glahms Oedipus Rex and produced a litter of just two, both peppers—a dog, Aust./N.Z. Ch. Jollygaze Golly Gosh, or "Amos," and a bitch, Jollygaze Gee Whiz, known as "Scarlett." Amos has sired well for Jollygaze, but to date none of his offspring is more famous than his pepper son, Aust. Grand/Am. Ch. Hobergays Fineus Fogg or "Harry," the top-winning Dandie in US history, but more on him later.

Betsy's last litter was by Paddy and produced Jollygaze Extra Special or "Delilah." A prolific brood bitch with litters of seven and eight puppies free whelped, she is the dam of Jollygaze Keeping Faith, known as

"Fiona," who has come to America and lives at the Arkansas branch of King's Mtn. with Vern and Anne Wilson, and Ch. Jollygaze His Majisty, called "Albert," a pepper dog owned by Rhonda Davis in Ohio.

Another litter of interest is one sired by Aust. Grand/ Am. Ch. Hobergays Fineus Fogg out of King's Mtn. Grace Note, a litter of six which has produced Jollygaze Spellbound or "Sinclair," Jollygaze Sugar Plum Fairy and Aust. Ch. Jollygaze Serendipity, called "Sid." Sinclair has already produced Jollygaze Time Lord or "Kevin," an exciting mustard dog out of Hobergays Importance.

DANDIES IN NEW ZEALAND

The New Years Day 1996 Best in Show win in Australia by Aust. Ch. Borderstone Dawn Dancer caught the attention of Mrs. Josie Whittall of New Zealand and prompted her to call Emma

Aust. Ch. Dandiedale Rupert Bear, better known as "Paddy."

Aust. Ch. Borderstone Dawn Dancer, the foundation bitch at Jollygaze kennels, imported from the UK. She goes by "Betsy."

Greenway in Australia. It was the start of a very successful collaboration until Mrs. Whittall's death in 2004.

Josie, as a teenager in England in the 1940s, had owned Dandies and had even bred a litter that contained a most notable bitch, Hobergays Jenny, who figured prominently in the pedigrees of some of the imports to America in the 1950s.

Upon emigrating to New Zealand in 1952, Josie found herself unable to acquire a worthy Dandie so instead bred Labrador Retrievers with great success. Unable to get Dandies out of her system, Josie finally imported some from the UK and Australia in the 1980s and bred them under the prefix "Kringle." Largely disappointed with the overall quality she was producing, she ceased her breeding program again and did not restart until the early 1990s. To mark her new beginnings she reregistered her kennel, returning to her original prefix "Hobergays."

Starting again, Josie imported Betic

Dulcamara or "Kizzy" from the UK. She had bred Kizzy once to imported semen from Eng. Ch. Renald Ulysses, producing a litter of five. The four males Josie deemed not sound enough for further use but she kept the one bitch who met her standards, Hobergays Besom. It was at this point that Josie made her first trip to Australia and the relationship between Hobergays and Jollygaze began in earnest.

After Josie's first visit to Jollygaze, Kizzy was sent to Australia and bred to Aust. Ch. Jollygaze Arising Sun. She produced a litter of four, including N.Z. Ch. Hobergays Changeling. Josie's first visit to Australia coincided with the birth of the Jollygaze "B" litter. Since there were no viable stud dogs in New Zealand, Jollygaze Baltizar Dawn would pay an extended visit to New Zealand, arriving in late 1996. "Edward" at ten months of age won Best in Show there at a terrier specialty show under Old Iron Airedale breeder and judge Mrs. Anne Sorraghan. Edward was then put

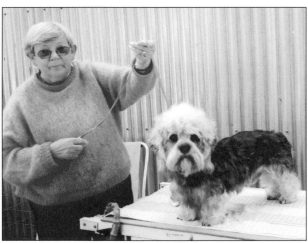

THE AUTHOR MEETS JOSIE AND KIZZY

The author judged in New Zealand in July 2004 and made a separate trip to Palmerston North to visit Josie at the nursing home where she would live out her days. I arrived early in the morning to find the entire nursing home informed of my visit and Josie sitting up in her chair, breakfasted and waiting. We spent a lovely morning talking Dandies, looking at her carefully constructed photo album and talking about how lucky we both were to have two young women in our lives who would carry on our breeding plans long after we were gone, a comfort few breeders have. Josie had a surprise planned for me. Much to my delight, the famous Kizzy came bursting through the door for a visit. Kizzy is famous around the Dandie world for her escapades Josie had written about. Sadly, Josie died not quite three weeks after my visit.

to Hobergays Besom to produce an important litter, which included the pepper bitch Hobergays Dream Dancer and the mustard dog Hobergays Drummer Boy.

Edward returned to Jollygaze and to replace him, Jollygaze sent Aust. Ch. Jollygaze Golly Gosh. Amos was put to Hobergays Dream Dancer and produced an impressive litter, including Aust. Grand/Am. Ch. Hobergays Fineus Fogg, Aust. Ch. Hobergays Humdinger and Hobergays Fiesty O Fife.

Amos was then put to N.Z. Ch. Hobergays Besom and produced

Hobergays Gadabout or "Giles" and Aust. Ch. Hobergays Gussie Gumdrop.

Josie's last litter was only one puppy, by Amos and out of N.Z. Ch. Hobergays Changeling, a bitch named Hobergays Importance or "Connie." By this time Josie's illness was advancing, and she carefully placed all her breeding stock with her partner, Dr. Emma Greenway in Australia. If Josie and Emma had been co-breeding in America, their dogs would have carried both kennel prefixes, and they'd have been listed as co-breeders. However, that is not allowed in Australia or New Zealand, so while all of their breedings were the result of a collaboration, the kennel prefix tells us which puppy was born in which country.

A note must be made here about Hobergays Fineus Fogg, bred by Josie Whittall in partnership with his owner/handler Dr. Emma Greenway. Harry began his career in Australia as a youngster and garnered some nice wins along the way, but nothing compares to his career as a mature dog. As of September 2005, Harry had amassed 30 all-breed Bests in Show, including the Adelaide Royal as well as the

Aust. Ch. Borderstone Dawn Dancer and Aust. Ch. Dandiedale Rupert Bear.

Aust./N.Z. Ch. Jollygaze Baltizar Dawn, a sire of great significance Down Under and in the US.

Melbourne Royal not two weeks later, a feat not accomplished by any other dog in 40 years, along with 17 runner-up Bests in Show and 62 Groups. Since he'd done it all in his home country, it was decided he'd come to America and debut on the second day of the five-day Tucson, Arizona cluster in November 2005, which was also home of the 2005 DDTCA national specialty. The first day he was Reserve Winners Dog to an audible gasp from ringsiders. The second day he was Winners Dog and Best of Winners for his first five American points. The next day he was BOB out of the classes for his second set of five American points and on to first in the Terrier Group and then Best in Show in a lineup of some

Aust./N.Z. Ch. Jollygaze Golly Gosh at six months old. He is the sire of "Harry."

of America's top winners. The final day he repeated by winning BOB from the classes to finish his American championship, and he would go on to win the Terrier Group and another Best in Show. Fourteen weeks after Harry's first BIS he made Dandie history. Handled by Bill McFadden, Harry overtook Ch. Woodbourne Next In Line, called "Clark," whose record ten Bests in Show held for 29 years. Harry won BIS number 11 at Kings Kennel Club of California on March 4, 2006 under judge Mrs. Helen Lee James. Mrs. James was also the judge who awarded Harry his first BIS in the US at the Tucson show on November 21, 2005. Dr. Emma Greenway, along with new co-owners Capt. Jean L. Heath and Dr. William H. Cosby, continue to campaign Harry in the US, as he accumulates more top wins around the country.

THE AUSTRALIAN AND NEW ZEALAND INFLUENCE IN AMERICA

After the author's first visit to Australia in 1998, semen was imported from Hobergays Drummer Boy and put to Ch. King's Mtn. Pixie Montizard, resulting in a litter of five of which two were shown to their titles: the mustard dog Ch. King's Mtn. Krokadile Dandie or "Hogan," and the mustard bitch Ch. King's Mtn. Pardon Me Boys or "Priscilla." She was handled by the late Bob LaRouech. Hogan enjoyed a quick campaign to his title, finishing in five successive shows. Priscilla was bred back to her great-grandsire Ch. Pennywise King's Mtn. MVP to produce Ch. King's Mtn. Bentley. Bentley's littersister, King's Mtn. Grace Note, was sent to Jollygaze in Australia, where she is making her mark in the whelping box. Hogan is the sire of Ch. King's Mtn. Elsbeth Elfwish, the foundation bitch for Sandra Wolfskill and Donna Francis in Ohio. Elfwish is well known around the world for the success of their Pembroke Welsh Corgis.

Pixie was next bred to frozen semen from Aust./N.Z. Ch. Jollygaze Baltizar Dawn, Hobergays Drummer Boy's sire, with a litter of four resulting, two of which became champions. The two are the pepper bitch Ch. King's Mtn. Good Grief!, owned by Merlyn and Susan Green, and the mustard bitch Ch. King's Mtn. Mouse Trap, who was Best of Opposite Sex at the 2004 DDTCA national specialty, handled by Sandra Pretari.

Pixie was next put to frozen semen from Aust. Ch. Jollygaze Arising Sun, a half-brother to Baltizar Dawn. This was a breeding that fascinated Emma Greenway and me; since

Gordon's and Pixie's photographs were virtually interchangeable, we were breeding like phenotypes hoping for a good bitch from this combination. We were rewarded with Ch. King's Mtn. Cordelia, shown by her co-owner, Miriam Couto.

Other breeders in America have used several of the Australian stud dogs with success. Cathy Nelson used Ch. Jollygaze His Majisty, producing Ch. Pennywise Gilded Lily. Linda Winfrey used Aust./N.Z. Ch. Jollygaze Baltizar Dawn to produce two champions: Ch. Glengarry Joey and Ch. Glengarry Waltzing Mathilda.

Ch. King's Mtn. Mouse Trap produced the first litter in America by Aust. Grand/Am. Ch. Hobergays Fineus Fogg. A litter of six with two impressive champions, Ch. King's Mtn. Stuart Little, handled by co-breeder/co-owner Sandra Pretari, and Ch. King's Mtn. Minnie Mouse, handled by her co-owner, Don Watkins. A third from this litter, King's Mtn. Godiva, called "Truffles," is their pepper sister and lives with her co-owner, Vern Wilson.

Aust. Grand/Am. Ch. Hobergays Fineus Fogg, the top-winning Dandie in history.

Aust./N.Z. Ch. Jollygaze Arising Sun is the half-brother to Aust./N.Z. Jollygaze Baltizar Dawn.

Paul Keevil, an eccentric English art dealer, and his famous Dandie "Crosby" are a winning look-alike duo in the UK. Paul's gallery specializes in dog-related items and is called Canine Art Connections.

CHARACTERISTICS OF THE

DANDIE DINMONT TERRIER

LIVING WITH A DANDIE

The Dandie is the gentleman of the terrier group, more placid and quiet than most of his terrier cousins. He is relatively calm and sensible, quite placid unless his "terrier" is aroused. At that point he becomes all-terrier and will pursue whatever interests him with tenacity.

The Dandie is a companion dog par excellence; to his fans he has no equal. He thrives on being with those he loves and doesn't take kindly to being locked away; he is a miserable kennel dog. A well-socialized Dandie taken everywhere from the time he's very young will grow into a most reliable canine companion. I often think of them as a person in a fur coat—those eyes, that look. They have a special ability to read your mind and mood, adapting to being exactly the kind of dog to suit the moment. Dandie Dinmont Terriers who grow up with a noisy young family will often be more spirited than those who grow up as a companion to an older person living alone. That is not to say that one situation is preferable over the other, but you will see a difference.

The Dandie is the self-appointed head of the welcoming committee of your household. When any member of

his family arrives home, he rushes to the door with a little conversation and the whole of his being wagging. After a few pats and cuddles, he is content to lie in his bed watching, with one eye open, not missing any move you make. He will be resting quietly by your side, but the moment you get up to do something he will be at your heels to help you with whatever it is you're going to do. The same applies to your guests. All should expect an enthusiastic greeting lasting about ten minutes and then the Dandie disappears to his bed or special

Ch. King's Mtn. Norton, bred by the author, is a one-dog welcoming committee! Owners, Vern and Anne Wilson.

Father and son "Paddy" and "Gordon" know how to cool off on a hot day. Whether pup or adult, Dandies are fun-loving, energetic, personable dogs.

corner. Dandies love to be under something, often making the spot under a coffee or corner table their own. As your guests bid you good-bye, your Dandie will appear out of nowhere and see them to the door. No Dandie thinks of himself as anything but a fully fledged member of the family.

By now you know the Dandie's eyes and expression could melt a heart of stone. These creatures with their big round dark brown eyes and crowning topknot appear to be angelic. They are some of the time, but these are not ladies' lap dogs. They are real dogs who need an alpha owner but with a soft touch, as the Dandie is a big dog in a small package.

Dandies are puppies for the first year, and for the next 12 months they are typical teenagers, enthusiastic about everything they like to do, boisterous, energetic and full of themselves, not too different from two-legged teenagers. It is during this

time that your Dandie will require your firm but loving touch. At about three to four years of age, the Dandie becomes a calm, sensible and responsible member of the household who can be trusted to remember what it is you like and what you dislike.

Dandie puppies should attend puppy kindergarten, special classes set up for puppies between 16 weeks and 6 months of age where they learn the basics of obedience training. They learn to walk nicely by your side, sit and lie down on command, come when they're called, well...maybe. Dandies are notorious for hearing you call them but continuing to do what they are doing at the time as if to say, "Yes, I hear you but I'll be another minute or two." After graduating from kindergarten, it is best to carry on with the Novice beginning obedience course, designed for dogs 6 to 12 months of age. Your Dandie will never be the star of the class, preferring to leave the precision obedience work to those breeds who enjoy it, but he will learn well enough to please you. This is not to say that Dandies can't qualify for obedience titles, as they can and do, it's just they're not the breed selected by diehard obedience enthusiasts. A person who enjoys obedience training Dandies for competition is obviously equipped with a marvelous sense of humor and a gift for keeping training sessions enjoyable and entertaining for both man and dog.

Agility, rally and flyball are new sports in the dog world, stealing participants away from the precision obedience world to the fun of agility trials. Some Dandies are enjoying the challenges and becoming proficient.

Dandies like looking their best and, while they may not always admit it, they do enjoy their bath and grooming. The weekly nail clipping is an exercise in "master dominating dog," a requirement through their youth and a subtle reminder that they are a d-o-g and you are the chief! Later in life, the Dandie enjoys the weekly grooming session and the good feeling that results from a stimulating warm bath, blow drying and brushing.

Dandies do well in pairs. If your dog is left home alone all day most days, then do consider two Dandies; they keep each other company and contented. Best is a male and a female, and obviously you will have them both fixed. Two females will work well together as long as they are spayed. Keeping two males, even neutered, is taking a chance that they will one day not get along, and it is not recommended.

If you're a cat lover, it's best that the Dandie puppy begin his life with you in the company of a cat. Bringing a new cat into the household run by an established Dandie is not recom- mended, as the moment the cat runs from the Dandie, natural instincts will flood his body and the chase is on. As soon as the dog has trapped and caught the cat a real brawl almost always results, with the cat usually coming out the big loser. I would

LIVING WELL INTO OLD AGE

Dandies leave middle age and become senior citizens at approximately seven to eight years of age. At this time it is best to include a geriatric blood panel in your Dandie's annual physical examination. By catching small problems early, they can be treated and hopefully help your Dandie live well into old age. Be sure to include the thyroid function in the blood panel, as hypothyroidism is a common ailment in older Dandies. Consult your veterinarian about diet, as it is generally recommended that older dogs have foods that are lower in protein and fat content, foods which are more easily utilized and digested. With a little luck and good care, your Dandie can be expected to reach 12 to 15 years of age.

never ask a Dandie to share his home with a ferret, guinea pig or hamster, as these little creatures are much too close to the breed's natural prey, and there would never be peace in the house.

Terrier trials testing the gameness of the Dandie have become quite popular in the United States; the American Kennel Club also sponsors earthdog trials where Certificates of Gameness are awarded. Dandie puppies are not particularly game, but as they mature their instincts develop, and many Dandies have met the requirements to earn Certificates of Gameness.

The Dandie is not naturally a guard dog but fulfills the job because of his big voice. From behind a closed door he sounds like a very big dog indeed. He is gifted with keen hearing and a curious nature, so a strange sound will rouse him from his bed in a flash to investigate. This is normally all the deterrence needed by a burglar, who—given the option—will usually move to a house without a noisy dog!

A big dog in a small body, the Dandie Dinmont is not easily intimidated. This Dandie has met a group of sheep who are equally curious about him.

THE IDEAL DANDIE HOME

As a companion to an adult or working couple, the Dandie is ideal provided that when his owner is home he is included in the household activities. The Dandie loves to accompany his owner on errands in the car, go for a walk around the town, through the woods or on the beach or visit a neighbor's home. Long motor trips are especially enjoyed, and any new adventures are fine as long as he gets to go along. He will be no trouble during the ride, usually content to sleep quietly on a rug on the back seat or confined in his travel crate, whichever you prefer.

The Dandie, like many other breeds, is a good choice for children. That said, it is important to add that puppies should meet infants and toddlers while they, too, are very young, as dogs are not always comfortable with very small humans if they haven't grown up with them. If you are seeking a pet for your young family, then acquiring the puppy at a young age is highly desirable. The Dandie puppy enjoys the play of young children but as a youngster he has a sharp row of puppy teeth himself and must be watched carefully that he not bite or nip when playing. An adult should always be watchful of a puppy and children playing together.

Dandies are baby-like for a longer period than most breeds. Ten to twelve weeks is an ideal age for a Dandie puppy to leave his breeder, dam and littermates and move to his

new home and family. It is at this age that the Dandie puppy can sleep quietly overnight in his crate and be clean in the morning, eat heartily out of his own dish without the competition of his littermates, respond to his name and take kindly to his first lessons, walking on collar and lead.

The young Dandie loose in the house needs to be watched. He can quickly become an electrician and chew up lamp cords, or a librarian interested in the tasty spines of books, or a woodworker, adding well-chiseled detail to the legs of chairs and tables. All Dandies need safe toys: plush toys to carry around and sleep with and toys to chew, including knotted ropes and special nylon chew bones.

If you are a working family with children away at school during the day, then special provisions need to be made to keep your Dandie safe and comfortable while he is on his own. The best solution is a kennel run outside designed especially for your dog, situated at the end of the yard or on the side of the house so it will not spoil the landscaping. The puppy will need protection from the elements in the form of a dog house, preferably with a wooden patio on the front for sunbathing, as Dandies love the sun. The best surface for a dog run is small gravel such as that used as roofer's gravel, and there is a reason for that. Dandies are notorious for digging and chewing—if they're going to swallow a rock, it's best that it be small and able to easily move through and be

SHOULD I BREED MY PET DANDIE?

Your children do not need to witness the miracle of birth by breeding their beloved pet. This knowledge can be gained by trips to the library for books and video tapes and DVDs on the subject. There are too many unwanted puppies in the world and unless your Dandie is of top show potential and has been specifically placed with you for breeding purposes, it is best to leave the breeding of Dandies to knowledgeable, committed, responsible breeders. While Dandies are relatively quite rare in all parts of the world, it is still a poor idea to breed from any stock that isn't of the highest quality in every respect.

dispelled without surgical assistance.

Dandies are naturally clean dogs, but you must provide them with enough space to be clean. Dogs like to do their business away from where

BREEDING TWO COLORS

It is customary to breed the two colors together, mustard and pepper. It is thought that good coat texture and pigment are best maintained when the two colors are bred together. Mustard is dominant and pepper is recessive, so by breeding mustard to pepper you can expect half the puppies to be mustard and half to be pepper. If mustard to mustard is bred, then three-quarters of the puppies are mustard and one-quarter are pepper. By breeding pepper to pepper, then all of the puppies will be pepper. Occasionally a puppy from a mustard to mustard breeding is homozygous mustard (carrying no pepper gene). Puppies with the pepper gene (from two mustard parents) have faint tan points above their eyes and around their anus. Breeders should make note of these puppies for future breeding plans.

they live and sleep, so their kennel must be large enough to accomplish this. The run should be a minimum of 4 feet wide by 25 feet long, but the larger the better. As is true of most earthdogs, Dandies love to dig, so it's best that the fencing be solid in the ground, as a Dandie is more likely to dig under a fence rather than go over it. Fencing 5 feet high will keep almost every Dandie in—climbers are rare.

Mature Dandies make good dogs for an apartment, but it would take an especially dedicated and watchful owner to raise a puppy in the city. The puppy would need to be walked every few hours, with one of those walks being brisk and long enough to constitute true exercise, and preferably give the puppy an opportunity for a really good romp in a park each day. I am not saying the Dandie can't be raised successfully in an apartment, only that it takes extra commitment and effort on the part of his owner.

The Dandie will seldom forget any special person in his life and will usually recognize his breeder after months, even years, of absence. Extremely loyal to his family, he can adapt to a new home and a new family if such a situation presents itself. If the new home makes him extremely welcome and the environment is a loving one, the Dandie will adapt.

MALE OR FEMALE?

Unless you are interested in breeding and showing, your concern lies with which sex will make the better companion. In reality, either will do very nicely, and the differences are subtle. I often describe the male Dandie as a little more carefree, and less intense than the bitch. He is a delightful and affectionate companion. I recommend that male Dandies going to pet homes be neutered at approximately 12 weeks of age. Veterinary science has proven that there are many benefits to early neutering of male dogs. Often early neutering precludes that time in a young male Dandie's life when he's going to test the waters so to speak, to see who is boss of the household, man or beast.

The female also makes a wonderful pet. However, she comes into season approximately every six months, and for a few weeks beforehand her hormones are raging and she can become cantankerous. Her season or estrous period will last about 21 days, during which time she will have a bloody vaginal discharge for the first week or so. It will lighten or stop while she ovulates and then start up again for the final few days. Unless you are interested in breeding her, these three weeks are most definitely inconvenient for all concerned. Special panties for bitches in season, available through pet-supply shops, help as far as keeping your premises clean and odor-free, but the bitch still needs to be watched to ensure she is not mistakenly mated. Dogs can be innovative and overcome the most amazing obstacles to romance.

Only the very best of stock should be bred from, so unless your dog or bitch is of superior quality, and only a very few truly are, you should spay or neuter your pet. The advantage to the male is the elimination of any

possibility of prostate cancer as the dog grows older. About the only difference you will notice is your dog does not exhibit any macho behaviors such as mounting the leg of your guest or marking your furniture.

Spaying the bitch ensures that she is sweet and loving, as she almost always is. A bitch who has never had a season will never have to face mammary cancer, whereas a bitch who has had one season will face a small risk. The removal of her uterus will ensure she never suffers from pyometra, a not uncommon massive infection which can afflict older bitches if their uterus is left intact after their reproductive days are over. Most experts recommend all bitches be spayed if they are not being used for breeding and I heartily agree. Veterinary science recommends that bitches not being used for breeding benefit from being spayed at approximately five months of age.

Regardless of your Dandie's sex, he or she will make an entertaining, affectionate companion.

THE GREAT WATER HUNTER

BY JOSIE WHITTALL

*The author is delighted to include this
classic "Kizzy adventure" from one of the
great Dandie doyennes. It was written many
years ago under the title "The Seal Hunt"
and still speaks volumes about our breed's
character.*

I have always been crazy about the sea.
Not to be on it, but to live beside it and
haunt the beaches. To know the tide, the sea
birds, and the shells and where the best
driftwood is to be found. For the past 20
years we have lived in close proximity to the
sea, but our latest move brought us to a
wilder coastline, open to the Tasman Sea,
with no sheltering islands and nothing
between our shoreline and the eastern coast
of Australia 2,000 miles away as the
albatross flies.

My Dandies also love the beaches and
we have spent many happy hours exploring
the open sands, me looking over the latest
magic carpet of marine flotsam carefully
unrolled by the last tide. The Dandies
looking along the high-tide mark for
anything dead or smelly that they can either
eat or roll in!

Hunting rabbits in the sandhills was
great fun until it got out of hand and I had to
put it out of bounds. In the summer it was
alright. Kizzy would disappear in the
sandhills, but I always knew where she was.
Because the sand in the hills became too hot
for comfort, and every 10 minutes or so she
would emerge with dangling tongue to rush
into the sea to cool off, before once more
returning to the hunt. The winter was a
different matter and hours would pass
without a sign of her, and when the
Conservation Department laid poison for
rabbits in the area, that was the end of that
little pastime.

Fur seals migrate along the coastline,
and in the spring inexperienced juveniles
can sometimes be seen weakened by lack of
food. The weaning of young seals is a
heartless business: mother seal just does not
return one day and the young seal must
learn to get out and hunt for himself or
starve to death.

Our first encounter with a seal was some
two years earlier, when I spotted a juvenile
atop a huge tree stump which had been
washed in by the tide. He had obviously
been resting there sunning himself as the
tide went out and had decided to wait until
the next high tide. The seal was well out of
reach of the Dandies and as he was not in
their line of vision they were oblivious of his
presence. I watched to see what would
happen. They snuffled their way along the
beach turning over every likely piece of
driftwood or pumice and were almost past
when they caught his scent—it was the most
perfect canine "double take" I have ever
seen. They stopped dead in their tracks. This
was certainly a scent they did not recognize!
Hackles went up and low growls were
emitted as they sniffed the air. Still unable to
spot the culprit but sure of some unknown
danger they were taking no chances. They
continued warily on their way with stiff gait
and rigid tails. I chuckled when I saw them

whip round suddenly to defend their rear ends from ambush.

It was the following spring when Clover (Kizzy's daughter), chasing seagulls on the beach, almost tripped over a young seal, imitating a log, lying in the shallows. I don't know who was more surprised. As the seal flip flopped his way into the sea, she gave instant chase, raising the Dandie alarm and swimming far out into the sea in hopeless pursuit. Kizzy was fussing around questing, trying to identify the quarry, but Clover was in no doubt; she had recognized the scent and now knew what creature she was after.

Now it was spring again, bright and sunny, the air cool and clear like champagne. The snow capped mountains range behind, the sparkling sea in front. "What a magic day," I thought as I parked the car on the sands above the high-tide mark. The dogs spilled out of the car in high spirits and were more than usually excitable. Clover started running up and down the beach like a whirling dervish, barking threats at the sea, and then she and Kizzy swam off through the breakers in a most determined fashion. This was unusual behavior; I became quite concerned and called them back. Then I spotted him...quite close in. A big black Granddaddy fur seal, nosing his way in through the breaker. Then, as I watched, he casually turned on his back with one flipper in the air in the most disarming manner, as if waving to the dogs. "Catch me if you can?" he seemed to say, as, rolling over he disappeared from view.

The Dandies had seen him too. They were incensed, screaming invectives into the wind, and they gave instant chase, charging through the breakers and heading out to sea in great style. By now I was really concerned, weak juvenile seals are one thing but Big Daddy seal himself was an entirely different kettle of fish, so to speak. Even in play he could bite or drown my intrepid pair in a flash. My cries went unheeded as they breasted one wave after another, determined to catch this cheeky fellow. Well, "Australia here they come," I thought, as their little heads disappeared from view. I was distraught, as I stood helpless on the deserted beach. Seconds seemed like hours as I watched the sea for a glimpse of them, and indeed I wondered if I would ever see them again. Finally two little waterlogged Dandies came into view and struggled ashore, but they were not at all dismayed. They then proceeded to race up and down the shallows at high speed, scenting the air and looking for some other way to gain access to their quarry. I was amazed that they could obviously air-scent him from so far out and in the sea.

As they sped up and down past me I was finally able to intercept them one by one and drag them protestingly to the car, still screaming defiance at the sea. Once I had them safely corralled in the car, I looked back. Big Daddy was there nosing his way closer in to the shore again: it was obviously a great game. He was still lying nonchalantly on his back rocking with the waves as I drove away, with two disgruntled Dandies giving me dirty looks from the back seat.

As I remarked to my friend later, "Well, of course Dandies are water hunters, but the Tasman Sea is hardly Eslington Pond and it was rather an oversize otter!"

WHAT ABOUT BACK PROBLEMS?

Long-backed dogs built low to the ground are often predisposed to vertebral disc disease. Breeds such as the Dachshund and Poodle are known particularly to suffer from chronic back problems, sometimes severe enough to cause paralysis.

The Dandie, as you've probably noticed from the photographs, has a natural arch over the loin area of his long back, different from the straight, rigid topline of his cousin, the Dachshund. This arch over the loin gives his back flexibility, a suppleness not seen in most other breeds of his short-legged class. Severe back problems are not common in the breed, although common sense dictates that precautions be taken in your care of the Dandie and his back.

Dandies should always be kept trim, lean and hard, like a well-tuned

King's Mtn. Elsbeth, a therapy dog at eight months of age. Owner, Dorothy Fletcher.

athlete. You do your dog no favor by fattening him up or allowing him to become a "couch potato," letting his muscles turn to jelly. Strong muscles through regular sensible exercise help to keep a dog in healthy condition everywhere, the back included. Dogs do not naturally become obese; that happens as a result of an overindulgent owner who cannot resist those pleading dark brown eyes. "But he looks so hungry," you say. As with humans, just because you're hungry does not mean you constantly eat. Between-meal snacks make dogs fat just as they do their owners!

A Dandie should be lifted into the car instead of being asked to jump in on his own. By putting one hand under his chest and supporting his long back and hindquarters with your other hand, you can safely lift your dog in and out, up and down. Dandies should not be encouraged to jump up and down from the sofa or bed and should avoid all situations that can aggravate a back that may not be inherently strong.

Symptoms of back pain are many and include a reluctance to go up and down stairs, lack of appetite, shivering and hiding. In the extreme, weakness in the hindquarters can lead to paralysis if left untreated. If you suspect a neck or back problem, see your veterinarian immediately. The use of chiropractors and massage therapists, those specially trained to work with animals, has proven a huge benefit in keeping the Dandie spinal column healthy. There are a number of

EAR PROBLEMS

Dandies have drop ears. Because the ear leather hangs by the cheek and covers the ear orifice, air does not circulate as easily down into the ear as it does with prick ears. It is important then to keep the canals as open as possible and pull hair from the ear canals, using your thumb and forefinger. Careful use of tweezers in the outer area only is permitted as long as you are careful not to enter the inner ear, as you could easily cause damage doing so. Dogs who shake their ears repeatedly or scratch at their ears with their back feet require veterinary attention. Ears should smell clean and fresh. Ears that have an unpleasant odor emitting from them need attention from a veterinarian. It is best not to guess what the problem is and experiment with home treatment, as there are many causes that require different solutions. Ear problems can easily become chronic, so it's important to get an accurate diagnosis and to follow it up with treatment as recommended and persist until all symptoms have completely disappeared.

Dandie breeders, exhibitors and pet owners too who routinely seek this kind of care for their dogs.

EYE DISEASES

Three minor eye conditions are seen occasionally in the breed. The most common is epiphora or watery eyes, producing excessive tearing and leaving a brown stain in the area of the eyes and down the sides of the muzzle. This most often is caused by inadequate tear drainage and is usually helped by flushing the nasolacrimal drainage system, which is a minor treatment performed by a veterinarian.

Another condition is corneal ulcer, which generally begins as a small scratch by a cat or a foreign object. Ulceration produces a cloudy appearance in the affected portion of the eye. The eye causes the dog pain and is frequently held shut. A thin, watery discharge, which later becomes purulent, is also present. Ulcers should be treated as soon as possible to relieve pain and prevent more serious complications.

Cherry eye is an eye in which the tear gland on the inner surface of the third eyelid prolapses, becoming visible in the inner corner of the dog's eye as a red cherry-like growth. This is a condition frequently seen in another breed with a large round eye, the Cocker Spaniel. Antibiotics and anti-inflammatory drugs may help relieve a very mild case but surgery is generally necessary to permanently repair most cases.

More serious eye diseases such as glaucoma, cataracts and lens luxation have been known to occur in the breed. A good question to ask any breeder is the history of eye diseases in his breeding stock, as all dogs used for breeding should be examined first by a veterinary ophthalmologist to ensure they are free from inherited eye diseases.

DANDIE DINMONT TERRIER

As the breed's history tells us, breeders of the original Dandies met in 1875 to organize a club and in 1876 met again to set down in words what the club members and breeders felt best described the ideal Dandie Dinmont Terrier. These breeders were writing the first breed standard for the Dandie Dinmont Terrier. The original English standard was modified three times thereafter, in 1877, 1892 and 1901, and then reformatted in 1991.

The Dandie Dinmont Terrier Club of America (DDTCA) updated their standard in the late 1980s at the request of the American Kennel Club. The AKC was attempting to "standardize" all the standards. The DDTCA seized the opportunity to clarify the breed standard and fill in much of the missing information. The new standard was approved in 1991.

The Dandie Dinmont Terrier of the 21st century is essentially the same in appearance as the "Mustards and Peppers" who first appeared in the company of the gypsies of the Scottish-English Border country in the 18th century. It is the adherence by breeders to the written description of the ideal Dandie Dinmont Terrier, the breed standard, that has kept the breed true to type all these many years.

THE AMERICAN KENNEL CLUB STANDARD FOR THE DANDIE DINMONT TERRIER

The author's comments on the AKC standard, in *italics*, help the reader to understand what the standard intends and are geared toward exhibitors and judges alike.

General Appearance: Originally bred to go to ground, the Dandie Dinmont Terrier is a long, low-stationed working terrier with a curved outline. The distinctive head with silken top is large but in proportion to the size of the dog. The dark eyes are large and round with a soft, wise expression. The sturdy, flexible body and scimitar shaped tail are covered with a rather crisp double coat, either mustard or pepper.

Ch. Montizard King's Mtn. Kricket possesses dark round eyes, set well apart, and a head that would fill a judge's hand.

As a judge I look for the characteristics described in the General Appearance paragraph when I take that first look at a class of Dandies. I want to stand across the ring and see the correct silhouette, which is of a very long and low dog with what Dandie fanciers call a "weasely" (or shapely) outline. Long, low and weasely are the three words you should be thinking when you're looking at a Dandie. Walking down the row of dogs, looking at heads, I want to see large round dark eyes set wide apart, which would indicate to me that under the crowning topknot is a skull that will "fill my hand" upon closer examination. While the same size and weight applies to both dogs and bitches, I still want to see an obviously masculine dog and a feminine bitch.

There are three important elements of breed type that must be present:

- *Silhouette must be very long*
- *Silhouette must be a series of gentle curves in the right places*
- *Crowned with an impressive, distinctive head*

Size, Proportion, Substance: Height is from 8 to 11 inches at the top of the shoulders. Length from top of shoulders to root of tail is 1 to 2 inches less than

Long, low and "weasely" describe the outline of Ch. Montizard King's Mtn. Kricket, owned by Drs. Mark and Patrice Parker.

twice the height. For a dog in good working condition, the preferred weight is from 18 to 24 pounds. Sturdily built with ample bone and well developed muscle, but without coarseness. The overall balance is more important than any single specification.

What is described here is a low-stationed, very long dog with a lot of substance but without coarseness. We as judges try to interpret the breed standard as it was intended. We all bring a different background to judging, and as we move along it is the comparison of one breed to another that teaches us how to better interpret a standard. I think to properly

COMPARISON OF DESIRED OVERALL LENGTH FROM PROSTERNUM TO BUTTOCKS*

10-inch Skye Terrier	20 inches long
11-inch Cardigan Welsh Corgi	19 to 20 inches long
13-inch Glen of Imaal Terrier	21 to 22 inches long
11-inch Pembroke Welsh Corgi	21 to 22 inches long
11-inch Dandie Dinmont Terrier	26 to 27 inches long

* 6 inches has been added to the length based on the norm when measuring from the elbow and withers to the prosternum.

understand just how long a Dandie should be that it is helpful to compare its height and length to other breeds of the short-legged class: that is breeds where their standards are specific.

When the standard revision committee delved into the matter that few, if any, of the then-current Dandies actually measured close to the ideal measurements in the breed standard, we tried to see if changing where the Dandie was measured would be appropriate. We could find no historical documentation that supported measuring the Dandie anywhere but from the top of the shoulder blade, the withers. There was nothing to give us the excuse to measure the dog's length from the point of shoulder, the prosternum.

An 11-inch Dandie at the withers should measure 20 to 21 inches from that point back; then add approximately 6 more inches for a moderately well-angulated front assembly, measured from elbow to prosternum forward...so that a Dandie, with proper proportions, would measure at least 6 inches longer than a Skye Terrier! How often do you look out at the Terrier Group and see a Dandie as long as a Skye, let alone longer than a Skye?

I have seen a number of very long curvy Dandies whose outlines filled my

ACCORDING TO THEIR RESPECTIVE AKC STANDARDS

BREED	HEIGHT	LENGTH
Skye Terrier	10 inches	Measured from chest bone over tail at rump, 20 inches in overall length.
Cardigan Welsh Corgi	10 $\frac{1}{2}$ to 12 $\frac{1}{2}$ inches	1.8:1 proportions: for example, an 11-inch dog at the withers, when measured from prosternum to rear of hip (ischial tuberosity), will measure 19 to 20 inches long in overall length.
Glen of Imaal Terrier	12 $\frac{1}{2}$ to 14 inches	Measured from sternum to buttocks, a length-to-height ratio of approximately 5 to 3; meaning a 13-inch dog at the withers should be 21 to 22 inches in overall length.
Pembroke Welsh Corgi*	10 to 12 inches	Measured from withers to base of tail, approximately 40% greater, which means an 11-inch-tall dog should measure 15 to 16 inches long from withers to base of tail (plus approximately 6 more inches in length when including withers to prosternum).
Dandie Dinmont Terrier	8 to 11 inches	Measured from the withers to root of tail, twice the height, less 1 to 2 inches; an 11-inch-tall dog should measure 20 to 21 inches from withers to tail (plus approximately 6 more inches in length when including the distance from withers forward to prosternum).

* Thanks to Donna Francis and Sandra Wolfskill of the Elfwish Pembroke Welsh Corgis for these measurements.

Illustration of the ideal Dandie Dinmont Terrier, showing proper structure, proportion and balance.

eye, and I don't believe any one of them measured 26 to 27 inches in overall length. My point in this discussion is to make the case that when judging Dandies, emphasis must be made on correct proportions. Great length is coveted. You must remember this is a very long dog indeed.

I have judged large specialty entries of both the Skye Terrier and the Pembroke Welsh Corgi. In quality entries of both breeds, there is always an abundance of quality dogs of correct proportions to choose from. I cannot say the same for the Dandie breed as a whole. When the Dandie goes off type, it is almost always the proportions that suffer; the breed tends to get upright on leg with short cobby bodies.

Weight for the Dandie is 18 to 24 pounds, and historically the lower weights were preferred. The standard of excellence as taken from Charles Cook's book published in 1885 stated the desired weight was 14 to 24 pounds with 18 pounds being preferred. He wrote that the Dandie Dinmont Club "did wisely to restrict the maximum weight to 24 pounds—the weight to be aimed at being 18 pounds which allows a dog having plenty of bone and yet to be small enough for ordinary practical work. This refers to dogs in good working condition." Preference must be given to the dog who is within these weights provided the correct height to length and curvy outline are also present. Rewarding a weedy, cobby specimen because it is small is not desired.

Head: The head is strongly made and large, but in proportion to the dog's size. Muscles are well developed, especially those covering the foreface. The expression shows great determination, intelligence and dignity.

In a mature Dandie, look for the expression to be wise, rather than cute.

The eyes are large, round, bright and full, but not protruding. They are set wide apart and low, and directly forward. Color, a rich dark hazel. Eye rims dark.

The eyes are an important part of Dandie type. Most importantly the eyes should not appear buggy or protruding. The eye itself should be large. It should not appear large because someone has pulled a wide swath of hair out all around the eye rim, creating a wide goggle-eyed look, which gives a totally foreign expression. Some exhibitors even add a layer of blackened petroleum jelly to make these goggles stand out even more. This is unsightly. What exactly is a "rich dark hazel" color? If it occurs to you that the dog

appears to have a light eye, then the eye is obviously too light in color.

The ears are set well back, wide apart and low on the skull, hanging close to the cheek, with a very slight projection at the fold. The shape is broad at the base, coming almost to a point. The front edge comes almost straight down from base to tip; the tapering is primarily on the back edge. The cartilage and skin of the ear are rather thin. The ear's length is from 3 to 4 inches.

The ears frame the face. Thick ear leather is generally felt on ears that are too big and houndy. That said, I have never seen an entry of sufficient quality in this breed where the defining point was based on ear set or ear carriage. We are a long way from reaching that level of quality.

The skull is broad between the ears, gradually tapering toward the eyes, and measures about the same from stop to occiput as it does from ear to ear. Forehead (brow) well domed. Stop well defined. The cheeks gradually taper from the ears toward the muzzle in the same proportion as the taper of the skull.

The skull measures about the same from stop to occiput as it does from ear to ear. It is said the skull should "fill your hand." Do not expect the skull on a bitch to be as large as that of a dog. There is no way to feel for the correct skull without crushing the topknot. Your hands-on examination of the Dandie skull is a must. No matter, though, as a correct topknot will fluff right up again.

The Dandie's canine teeth should be "extraordinary" for his size. A complete scissors bite is desired in the Dandie.

The muzzle is deep and strong. In length, the proportions are a ratio of 3 (muzzle) to 5 (skull). The nose is moderately large and black or dark colored. The lips and inside of the mouth are black or dark colored.

Remember, this is not a short-faced breed. We want a muzzle of correct proportions, with good width at the cheek, which is what gives the muzzle the desired strength. You should not look at a muzzle and think it's cube-like in appearance nor should it be long and narrow or weak in the underjaw. The skull and the muzzle should be on a roughly parallel plane and certainly shouldn't appear either down-faced or upturned.

The teeth meet in a tight scissors bite. The teeth are very strong, especially the canines, which are an extraordinary size for a small dog. The canines mesh well with each other to give great holding and punishing power. The incisors in each jaw are evenly spaced and six in number.

A scissors bite with large teeth is desired. The incisors should be in a straight line set well into a strong jaw. Horseshoe-shaped jaws are usually found on weak narrow muzzles. I am surprised today at how many Dandies are found in the show ring with mouth faults, both undershot teeth and wry mouths. However, I would never reward an overall inferior dog with a perfect mouth over a clearly superior dog, one with the correct long curvy silhouette, with an obvious mouth fault.

You will find a number of Dandies in the ring who have, upon examina-

Illustration of an ideal Dandie Dinmont Terrier head, crowned with silken top.

tion, a rectangularly shaped skull, eyes too small and set too close together, not enough stop and a longish, narrow muzzle. This is a genetic package and these faults are almost always found together.

Neck, Topline, Body: The neck is very muscular, well developed and strong, showing great power of resistance. It is well set into the shoulders and moderate in length.

The neck is not stuffy, short, bull or thick nor is it overly long and thin. The correctly shaped neck has an arch to it. The transition from the neck into the body is smooth and fluid, indicating a well-laid-back and well-set-on shoulder blade.

The topline is rather low at the shoulder, having a slight downward curve and a corresponding arch over the loins, with a very slight gradual drop from the top of the loins to the root of the tail. Both sides of the backbone well muscled. The outline is a continuous flow from the crest of the neck to the tip of the tail.

The body is long, strong and flexible. Ribs are well sprung and well rounded. The chest is well developed and well let down between the forelegs. The underline reflects the curves of the topline.

The make and shape of the Dandie is an integral part of breed type and without it fanciers have long said, "No outline, no Dandie." This unique outline is the hallmark of the breed. Please note the key word in this description is "slight." The long, low stature has much in common with other breeds of the same class. The curvy nature of the breed has much in common with other curvy breeds, such as the Borzoi, the Whippet and especially the Scottish Deerhound. The curvy sighthound breeds finish differently over the croup, but their back and topline are also flowing and smooth with no bumps, lumps, dips or exaggerations.

Illustration of correct front and rear views.

To those who think the Dandie is more caricature than dog, they are sorely mistaken. The notion that everything that is wrong with other breeds is right with the Dandie is an ignorant statement and a total misconception.

Dr. M. Josephine Deubler in her February 1977 American Kennel Gazette *column wrote about the Dandie topline. She writes, quoting the standard of the times, "...the back rather low at the shoulder, having a slight downward curve and a corresponding arch over the loin, with a very slight gradual drop from top of loins to root of tail." She goes on to write, "The Dandie topline is a very important breed characteristic and 'slight' is a key word. There can be too much of a curve over the shoulder and a too highly developed loin, resulting in a faulty topline. The slight downward curve at the shoulder should match the slight arch over the loins. The very slight drop to the root of the tail produces another curve which corresponds to that over the shoulder. The whole topline has been described as a 'Hogarth S.' It all goes with a long, strong, flexible body."*

If on your examination of the Dandie on the table you feel the topline is flat, do not make that your final determination of the dog's topline. Make your final decision based on viewing the dog on the move, when viewed from the side. It is how the dog holds himself and looks when gaiting about the ring that is the final testament to its real shape.

The tail is 8 to 10 inches in length, rather thick at the root, getting thicker for about 4 inches, then tapering off to a point. The set-on of the tail is a continuation of the very slight gradual drop over the croup. The tail is carried a little above the level of the body in a curve like a scimitar. Only when the dog is excited may the tip of the tail be aligned perpendicular to its root.

The set-on of the tail is of utmost importance, as it is a continuation of the slight curves of the topline and provides the proper finish to the dog. The very slight gradual drop over the croup defines the tail set. Too steep a croup and the tail is carried low. With a flat croup the tail appears to come right off the back and will lack the proper finish. "In a curve like a scimitar" refers to the short, curved sword once used in the Middle East or by seafaring pirates. The tail should be carried somewhere between one and three o'clock when the dog is on the move. The sometimes electric atmosphere when a ring is full of mature males will elevate the tail carriage of most of the Dandies, so it is not uncommon to see the tail carried at twelve o'clock in these circum-stances. But as a judge I want to see the tail carried properly at least once during judging so I am assured that the dog possesses the desired tail set and carriage.

Forequarters: There should be sufficient layback of shoulder to allow good reach in front; angulation in balance with hindquarters. Upper arms nearly equal in length to the shoulder blades, elbows lying close to the ribs and capable of moving freely. The forelegs are short with good muscular development and ample bone, set wide apart. Feet point forward or very slightly outward. Pasterns nearly straight when viewed from the side. Bandy legs and fiddle front are objectionable.

The majority of the DDTCA membership, when voting on the standard revisions, did not approve the proposed language "well-laid-back shoulders." Dr. Deubler, a member of the standard revision committee, suggested that first sentence, which was ultimately approved. The English Kennel Club had already approved, "shoulders well laid back but not heavy," but we could not persuade the DDTCA membership to follow the lead of the country of the breed's origin. The upper arm "nearly equal" in length to the shoulder blade reads that way as it's a genetic impossibility for it to be the same length as the shoulder blade. Correctly angled Dandies will have their forelegs well under them, and a line can be drawn from the top of the withers through the elbow of the foreleg to the feet when viewing a correctly constructed front assembly from the side.

I place great emphasis on the correct front assembly, and I'm a very unhappy judge when I am forced to choose between an entire entry without a correct front. Since we judges are choosing breeding stock in our judgments, I personally would not breed from a dog or bitch who was straight in front, and I am loath to reward a dog who is inadequate in this area. This is a most complex assembly and once lost it's gone forever, no matter how many breedings are subsequently made to try and improve it. The correct front assembly assures proper head carriage, the slight arch to the neck, the smooth transition from the neck to the shoulders, carriage of the topline and, of course, good reach in front.

The original standard, as well as the revised English version, stayed with "immense muscular development and bone." We felt "good" muscular development and "ample" bone more in keeping with the meaning of those words in the late 20th century.

The correct front assembly is extremely similar, if not identical, to that of the Pembroke Welsh Corgi. The distance from elbow to ground is unusually short for the size of the dog. A dog that is high on the leg has overly long forearms and long hocks. When viewed from the front, the entire front assembly should not appear straight. The forearms turn in slightly due to shortness of leg in order to accommo-date the spring of rib and the depth of chest. The slight turn of the forearms make the wrists closer together than the elbows and shoulders. The pasterns and feet are parallel and point straight forward or very slightly outward. The so-called "terrier-straight" front lacks this characteristic slight turn in the forearm, and this widely misused term does not apply to the terriers of the short-legged class. "Terrier straight" refers to the front assemblies of the terrier breeds whose movement is pendulum-like, such as Airedales and Fox Terriers.

When examining the front assembly, your hand should cup a handful when feeling the prosternum, the prominent point of shoulder between the forelegs. If you put your hand there and feel nothing, where a seemingly straight line exists from throat to feet, then you can mentally dismiss this dog from further competition.

Hindquarters: The hind legs are a little longer than the forelegs and are set rather wide apart, but not spread out in an unnatural manner. The upper and lower thighs are rounded and muscular and approximately the same length; stifles angulated, in balance with forequarters. The hocks are well let down and rear pasterns perpendicular to the ground.

I have always felt that first sentence should read "The hind legs appear a little longer than the forelegs," as the correctly constructed Dandie should not appear stern high.

The hindquarters have a well-defined first and second thigh and good muscling on the inside as well as the outside of the thigh, which gives the Dandie's rear going away a well-rounded appearance. Coupled with well-angulated stifles and short hocks, the Dandie should drive well off his rear. There should be no evidence of sickle hocks, a common fault endemic in the Dachshund breed and seen more and more in the Dandie.

Feet: The feet are round and well cushioned. Dewclaws preferably removed on forelegs. Rear feet are much smaller than the front feet and have no dewclaws. Nails strong and dark; nail color may vary according to the color of the dog. White nails are permissible. Flat feet are objectionable.

Coat: This is a very important point: The hair should be about 2 inches long; the body coat is a mixture of about two-thirds hardish hair with about one-third soft hair, giving a sort of crisp texture. The hard coat is not wiry. The body coat is shortened by plucking. The coat is termed pily or pencilled, the effect of the natural intermingling of the two types of hair. The hair on the underpart of the body is softer than on the top.

The important thing to remember about the coat is texture, and there must be enough length to the coat and the proper mixture of soft undercoat to crisp outer coat so you may evaluate coat texture. "Sort of crisp texture" is exactly what should go through your

mind when you run your hands over the back of the Dandie. It should not feel wiry, nor soft and slick. Currently in the US few Dandies in the show ring are exhibited in much more than an inch of body coat.

The head is covered with very soft, silky hair, the silkier the better. It should not be confined to a mere topknot but extend to cover the upper portion of the ears, including the fold, and frame the eyes. Starting about 2 inches from the tip, the ear has a thin feather of hair of nearly the same color and texture as the topknot, giving the ear the appearance of ending in a distinct point. The body of the ear is covered with short, soft, velvety hair. For presentation, the hair on the top of the muzzle is shortened. The hair behind the nose is naturally more sparse for about an inch. The forelegs have a feather about 2 inches long, the same texture as the muzzle. The hind leg hair is of the same texture but has considerably less feather. The upper side of the tail is covered with crisper hair than that on the body. The underside has a softer feather about 2 inches long, gradually shorter as it

Illustration of correct coming and going on the move.

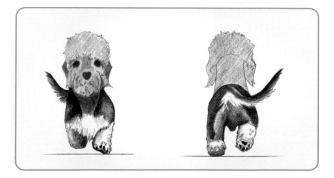

nears the tip, shaped like a scimitar. Trimming for presentation is to appear entirely natural; exaggerated styling is objectionable.

Color: The color is pepper or mustard. Pepper ranges from dark bluish black to a light silvery gray, the intermediate shades preferred. The topknot and ear feather are silvery white, the lighter the color the better. The hair on the legs and feet should be tan, varying according to the body color from a rich tan to a very pale fawn.

The newborn pepper Dandie is black and tan in the same coat pattern as that of the Doberman Pinscher or Manchester Terrier. As the puppy's coat grows, it begins to silver. Adult Dandies who have dark bluish black body coats will likely have rich tan legs and feet,

which is permissible. Adult Dandies who are lighter in body color will have very pale fawn legs and feet. Some exhibitors mistakenly try to make their dogs' legs and feet white.

Mustard varies from a reddish brown to a pale fawn. The topknot and ear feather are a creamy white. The hair on the legs and feet should be a darker shade than the topknot.

The newborn mustard Dandie is a very dark brown and unless there is a pepper puppy in the litter for comparison, many novice breeders believe these very dark brown puppies to be peppers. The depth of color in the mustard is sometimes inherited and other times is often due to coat management, or mismanagement if you will.

In both colors the body color comes well down the shoulders and hips,

Aust. Grand/Am. Ch. Hobergays Fineus Fogg, coming and going.

Illustration of correct side gait in the Dandie.

gradually merging into the leg color. Hair on the underpart of the body is lighter in color than on the top. The hair on the muzzle (beard) is a little darker shade than the topknot. Ear color harmonizes with the body color. The upper side of the tail is a darker shade than the body color, while the underside of the tail is lighter, as the legs. Some white hair on the chest is common.

Gait: Proper movement requires a free and easy stride, reaching forward with the front legs and driving with evident force from the rear. The legs move in a straight plane from shoulder to pad and hip to pad. A stiff, stilted, hopping or weaving gait and lack of drive in the rear quarters are faults to be penalized.

A properly constructed Dandie when viewed from the side should reach out well in front, hold his topline on the move with a noticeable slight arch over the loin and drive with evident force from behind. As speed increases there is a very slight inclination toward the center line of travel. Coming and going you will notice the tail acts as a rudder for balance.

Old-timers will refer to the "Dandie roll," which in more than 30 years in this breed I have never seen on a Dandie who was properly constructed. Certainly dogs who are not in good muscle tone, overweight or built too widely in front will roll to compensate for poor structure.

Of the three elements of gait, I place the greatest emphasis on the side gait, as there is very little reason for flawless coming and going if the dog cannot put it all together and cover ground smoothly, effortlessly and efficiently.

Temperament: Independent, determined, reserved and intelligent. The Dandie Dinmont Terrier combines an affectionate and dignified nature with, in a working situation, tenacity and boldness.

Approved February 9, 1991.

DANDIE DINMONT TERRIER

RECOGNIZING A RESPONSIBLE BREEDER

A responsible dog breeder will be interested in the life of the puppy he has bred for all of its long life; therefore, this person should be someone you like, come to know and feel comfortable with in contacting whenever you have a question or a problem, whether the dog is a young puppy or an aged veteran. Exercise your good common sense in evaluating a breeder, their home and environment for their puppies. There is nothing too complicated about breeding, showing and raising dogs, so the average person should understand the explanation. Thus if it sounds like doubletalk, it probably is. The talk should be straightfor-

Try to meet the dam of the litter when you're selecting your puppy.

DOG VERSUS BITCH

When deciding on the sex of your Dandie pup, here are a few points to consider. The standard for the Dandie dictates that the male and female are about the same size, between 18 and 24 pounds; however, most females will weigh between 19 and 22 pounds and males about 23 to 24 pounds. Like all breeds, the peacock syndrome holds true, with the male being more impressive in most ways, particularly in head, as he will generally have a bigger head with wider skull.

---

ward and your questions should be welcomed.

The premises should be clean and you shouldn't "smell dogs" as you go through the door. The adult dogs should be relatively clean, well groomed and social. Do remember the Dandies you've seen in the show ring have been groomed to the nines and it's a hair-do that lasts about 15 minutes. Most Dandies at home have their topknots flattened, their coats tousled and their beards grubby from running their noses along the ground to see what intruders might have visited their yard. Most Dandies are happy to meet new visitors to their home and give them an enthusiastic greeting.

Most breeders of Dandies operate on a very small scale and whelp only one or two litters each year. Litters are usually whelped in a quiet room of their home, and the puppies are raised in a home environment, not a kennel. Often the hobby breeder's best brood bitch is also their top show dog, as well as their house pet. The average size of a Dandie litter is four, and from that litter the breeder usually hopes that the best one or two puppies will go to show and breeding homes, with the remaining puppies being available as pets. Often when you're seeking to find a Dandie puppy to purchase as a pet, you will not have a choice of which puppy you might choose; instead, the breeder will point out the puppy that may be available to you if you pass muster!

Expect to be interviewed by the breeder and asked a myriad of questions. Common questions are:

- Why do you want a Dandie Dinmont Terrier? How did you learn about the breed? Have you ever seen one?
- Do you live alone or do you have a family? Are there children and, if so, what are their ages?
- Is someone at home during the day? If not, where will the puppy be kept while you're gone?
- Do you have a fenced yard? Is it "Dandie-proof"? If not, are you prepared to erect a proper dog run

Male or female, mustard or pepper? Be open-minded, as you will find a suitable companion faster.

where the puppy will be safe while you're away from home? Will the puppy be a house dog when you're home?

- Have you owned dogs before, and, if so, what kind? Do you have pets at home now? If so, what are they? Are your pets neutered?
- If not, why?
- What will you do with your dog when you go on vacation?
- Would you be willing to sign a contract that you won't breed your pet?

Responsible dog breeders will screen potential buyers vigorously and if they don't, you want to buy your Dandie puppy somewhere else.

HOW TO SELECT A DANDIE DINMONT PUPPY

Evaluating a litter of Dandies and their degree of socialization will depend on their age and whether just before you've arrived they've spent the previous hours running and playing. If that's the case, then nothing much can be done to wake them to perform for their visitors—

BE OPEN-MINDED

Dandies are among the rarest of the terrier breeds. Dandie litters are usually four or five puppies; litters of six or seven are not uncommon but unfortunately neither are litters of one or two puppies. Therefore it is best to be open-minded when looking to acquire a Dandie puppy and not limit your choice to a preferred color or sex.

they are tired and sleepy. This is when finding a responsible breeder becomes so important, as the breeder will know by instinct and experi-

ence from watching the litter all these weeks which puppy will suit which home. Puppies, like children, have slightly different personalities and temperaments, and within a litter the puppies will run the gamut. One puppy will be quite placid and content to sit for hours on a lap being cuddled. The other end of the spectrum will be a puppy who is busy, perky, wants only a couple of minutes worth of cuddles and then springs off your lap and on its merry way. Matching the right puppy to the correct home and situation is one of the special pleasures a breeder enjoys.

So how do you select your Dandie puppy? From what you've just read, you are now aware you will seldom have a choice of puppies, there being too few in this world for that luxury. It is best to be open-minded and consider a puppy of either color and either sex.

A word of caution: if you

A "triple-cute" litter of Dandies, seven weeks old, bred by Dr. Emma Greenway, known as the "B" litter.

already own a male dog, a Dandie or another breed, it is not recommended that you acquire a male Dandie puppy. All will be fine for the first six to nine months, but as he matures and reaches adolescence, trouble may begin brewing. The Dandie can be very possessive of his special people, and if there is jealousy there will also be competition for attention, affection and treats. An exception to this would be if your first dog is elderly, placid by nature and neutered. Two females, particularly if both are spayed, are generally a good combination. The best combination is one of each sex, the male being neutered and the bitch spayed.

All puppies are cute and Dandie puppies are triple cute. Their seemingly overly large skull is accentuated by the three-button look, two big round dark-colored eyes and a big piece of nose leather. Their body is long and low with big-boned legs and a very happy confident tail all wrapped up in a puppy coat that seems at once crisp but soft.

Dandie puppies are babies longer than most other breeds. They are often four weeks of age before they even dream of eating something from a dish and take several weeks to fully wean from their dam. Most Dandie mothers are exceedingly permissive and allow their puppies to nurse from them well into their third month of life.

According to dog behaviorists

and trainers, 49 days (7 weeks) of age is thought to be the optimal age when a puppy should leave his dam and littermates and move to his new home. This is the age when the pup will bond most easily to his new human family. This works for most breeds, but for the Dandie it is too soon. The optimal time for this breed is 10 to 12 weeks of age. At this time the Dandie puppy has learned to eat enthusiastically from his own dish, to sleep in his crate alone and be clean through the night. The 10-week-old is also learning to walk wearing a soft nylon buckle collar on a 6-foot leash. At this age he will move to his new home with a minimum of fuss and be an exceedingly well-adjusted puppy in his new home.

The puppy you are offered should be clean and fresh from a bath, well groomed and social. He should have bright clear eyes, with

The average litter size for the Dandie Dinmont is four puppies. Small litters of one or two puppies are not unusual, and occasionally there are litters of six to eight puppies.

On the move is Ch. Dunsandle Partridge MacPence, bred and owned by Miss France Roozen, shown here as a puppy.

Very young pups become accustomed to humans through the breeder's gentle petting and handling.

his topknot trimmed back so he sees the world clearly. The hair on his muzzle should be trimmed short so stray hairs are not sticking up into the eyes, irritating them. His nose should be cool and moist unless, of course, he's just been digging in the yard. His ear canals should smell clean and the hair should be plucked from the orifices. Up until four-and-a-half months of age, he will have his baby teeth. His toenails should be trimmed back so they are not clicking on the floor as he walks, and the hair between his toes should be trimmed short so the leather pads give him the necessary traction on linoleum and tile floors. The hair around his anus should be trimmed short and be free of any fecal matter. The body coat should be brushed and combed free of any tangles or mats, and you should return at a later date for a full grooming lesson on how you can trim your puppy to look like the Dandie he is.

PET VERSUS SHOW PUPPY

Certainly beauty is in the eye of the beholder and what one breeder deems as show and breeding quality, another breeder may believe is not of sufficiently high quality to be shown or bred. Only the best are retained for breeding purposes, and since dog shows are for the purpose of evaluating breeding stock, the words "show and breeding" are essentially synonymous. Since a breeder's continuing goal is to strive to improve the breed with every litter, the best pups are either retained or placed in homes for breeding purposes, and the remaining puppies are available as companions and pets.

Many new dog owners wonder what exactly makes a puppy pet quality as opposed to one who is deemed of show and breeding quality. Most often these faults are subtle and difficult for the average

pet owner to see. Some of the faults might be: eye color is a little light; the alignment of the jaw is off, resulting in a reverse scissors bite or slightly undershot bite; the muzzle may be long and narrow; the angle of the shoulder blade and upper arm is not sufficient; the front legs may rotate out more than desired; the arch over the loin may be more over the back or the rump; the angle of the croup may result in the tail being carried too gaily; and the coat may be too soft or the furnishings too sparse. These are only a few of the possible conformational flaws, but none of them detracts from the dog's overall suitability as a good-looking representative of his breed and companion par excellence.

SELECTING A SHOW AND BREEDING PROSPECT

First and foremost, you must come to know a knowledgeable breeder and that person must know you can be entrusted with one of these rare and valuable top-quality puppies. While you expect the breeder to place a top puppy with you, in turn that breeder must have the assurance that your interest in the breed is not a passing fancy and you are committed to becoming involved in the breed past pet ownership. This breeder will act as your mentor for the next five to ten years, and you will learn quite a bit about Dandies. It takes more than just a good specimen to make a winning dog, and how you socialize, groom and

present your Dandie will have almost as much to do with success in the ring as will the puppy's type, structure and movement. There is more to this sport of dogs than meets the eye.

Purchasing a show-prospect Dandie puppy means you will not be taking home a tiny puppy. A Dandie puppy at 12 weeks of age has only "show potential," and a great deal can go wrong during the next three months of growing

Trust your breeder's advice when evaluating a potential show puppy.

despite the puppy's obvious potential at a young age. If all good-looking 12-week-old puppies turned into top-flight show dogs, then breeding truly good dogs would be simple. It isn't.

A puppy bought for the express purpose of showing and breeding should be at least six months old. I look for the skull to be domey and blocky in appearance; it should "fill the hand," have a good amount of stop and a strong muzzle. The proportion of muzzle to skull is 3 to 5. The eyes will appear large and round and be dark hazel in color. The adult teeth will have erupted and they will be large, white, properly aligned and meeting in a scissors bite. The ears are set on low and frame the face. The head and top of the ears are covered with a silky textured topknot. Avoid a puppy where the muzzle appears overly short: the correct muzzle to skull proportions is what gives the proper adult expression, which is wise rather than cute. Avoid skulls that appear long, narrow and almost rectangular; usually they are coupled with long narrow muzzles with little stop and small eyes placed too closely together.

The proportions of height and length of body are of paramount importance. The body length is measured at the top of the shoulders (the withers) and should be "twice as long as he is tall, less 1 to 2 inches," a very long dog indeed. I like to see a puppy who appears long and lean with an almost arrow-like look, as this puppy will not become coarse and be overdone at maturity. Avoid puppies that appear almost short-bodied and cobby, as these will never lengthen to be long enough.

The body shape is unique and, along with the distinctive head, is a hallmark of the breed. It is described as long, low and weasely. The American Kennel Club standard includes a wonderful sentence about topline and outline, "The outline is a continuous flow from the crest of the neck to the tip of the tail." Avoid a puppy whose curves are in the wrong places and

At three weeks and three days old, it is much too early to tell what Gordon will look like when he grows up. A pup's true show potential cannot be evaluated until at least six months of age. He grew up to become Aust./N.Z. Ch. Jollygaze Arising Sun.

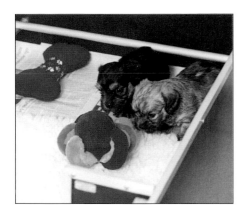

whose topline is lumpy and bumpy, as this puppy will not have the desired continuous flowing topline desired in the adult.

The tail is set on a very slightly sloping croup and carried in the shape of a scimitar, and held at about two or three o'clock. A puppy whose tail is set on a flat croup and is held at twelve or one o'clock makes an unattractive picture, and the flat croup will affect his ability to drive from behind. A highly held and carried tail will not correct with maturity. The shoulder blade is angled well back and balanced, with the upper arm angulation placing the forelegs well back under the body. When you run your hand down the front of a Dandie, you should feel the point of shoulder well out in front. The front legs are straight for a digging terrier, but not straight as compared to the long-legged terriers (such as the Airedale or Welsh). The Dandie front is commonly called the wrap-around front. Avoid a puppy with straight

shoulders and little upper arm angulation and nothing out in front. This is a major fault that will haunt a breeder's line forever.

The rear quarters of the puppy should show a well-developed first and second thigh, a well-rounded behind and short straight hocks. Sufficient angulation in front and rear enables the puppy to reach out well in front with evident drive from behind. Avoid puppies with narrow behinds and straight stifles. There should be no indication of a hock joint that will not flex, commonly called sickle hocks, a common fault in the breed.

The body is covered with a coat that is one-third undercoat and two-thirds crisp outer coat. A perfectly balanced coat is seldom seen and, if I had to choose a puppy with less than perfect coat, I would err on the side of a crisper body coat with fewer furnishings rather than choose a puppy who has profuse coat and cottony furnishings. The

Breeders usually allow prospective owners to visit the litter before the pups are old enough to leave. This also gives the owners a chance to see the breeders' facilities, to make sure the area is clean and to see that the pups are well cared for.

These adorable Dandie siblings look as if they might be able to cause just a little bit of mischief!

Pups learn a lot by interacting with their littermates. These Dandie siblings look to be the best of friends!

latter is a nightmare for both the pet owner and the breeder-exhibitor to groom and maintain. A well-trimmed Dandie with proper outgoing temperament and engaging personality can make a formidable show dog.

YOUR DANDIE SHOPPING LIST

Just as expectant parents prepare a nursery for their baby, so should you ready your home for the arrival of your Dandie pup. If you have the necessary puppy supplies purchased and in place before he comes home, it will ease the puppy's transition from the warmth and familiarity of his mom and littermates to the brand-new environment of his new home and human family. You will be too busy to stock up and prepare your house after your pup comes home, that's for sure! Imagine how a pup must

feel upon being transported to a strange new place. It's up to you to comfort him and to let your little pup know that he is going to be happy with you!

FOOD AND WATER BOWLS
Your puppy will need separate bowls for his food and water. Stainless steel pans are generally preferred over plastic bowls since they sterilize better and pups are less inclined to chew on the metal. Heavy-duty ceramic bowls are popular, but consider how often you will have to pick up those heavy bowls! Buy adult-sized pans, as your puppy will grow into them before you know it.

THE DOG CRATE
If you think that crates are tools of punishment and confinement for when a dog has misbehaved, think again. Most breeders and almost all trainers recommend a crate as the preferred house-training aid as well as for all-around puppy training

COST OF OWNERSHIP
The purchase price of your puppy is merely the first expense in the typical dog budget. Quality dog food, veterinary care (sickness and health maintenance), dog supplies and grooming costs will add up to big bucks every year. Can you adequately afford to support a canine addition to the family?

and safety. Because dogs are natural den creatures that prefer cave-like environments, the benefits of crate use are many. The crate provides the puppy with his very own "safe house," a cozy place to sleep, take a break or seek comfort with a favorite toy; a travel aid to house your dog when on the road, at motels or at the vet's office; a training aid to help teach your puppy proper toileting habits; and a place of solitude when non-dog people happen to drop by and don't want a lively puppy—or even a well-behaved adult dog—saying hello or begging for attention.

A medium-size crate will be necessary for a full-grown Dandie, who can stretch out quite long when his body is fully extended. The author prefers a Vari-Kennel made of high-strength copolymer plastic with an electro-welded steel door and side ventilation grills. The size preferred is the Medium, Model 200, measuring 20 inches wide by 27 inches long by 19 inches high. A large adult male requires the Model 300.

BEDDING FOR THE DANDIE

Soft bedding in the dog's crate will help the dog feel more at home. My preference is an old terry towel on the bottom topped with a synthetic imitation lambswool, of the same size as the crate. Small puppies often wet in their crates overnight and this combination of bedding allows the urine to go through the lambswool, which will remain dry in spite of the accident and be sopped up by the toweling. Crate bedding should be checked every morning and replaced if soiled.

Soft toys make playtime and socialization much more interesting.

With love, attention and a cozy place to call his own, your Dandie should settle into his new home in no time.

Puppy Toys

Just as infants and older children require objects to stimulate their minds and bodies, puppies need toys to entertain their curious brains, wiggly paws and achy teeth. A fun array of safe doggie toys will help satisfy your puppy's chewing instincts and distract him from gnawing on the leg of your antique chair or your new leather sofa. Most puppy toys are cute and look as if they would be a lot of fun, but not all are necessarily safe or good for your puppy, so use caution when

you go puppy-toy shopping.

Although Dandies are not known to be voracious chewers like many other dogs, they still love to chew. The best "chewcifiers" are nylon and hard rubber bones, which are safe to gnaw on and come in sizes appropriate for all age groups and breeds. Be especially careful of natural bones, which can splinter or develop dangerous sharp edges; pups can easily swallow or choke on those bone splinters. Veterinarians often tell of surgical nightmares involving bits of splintered bone, because in addition to the danger of choking, the sharp pieces can damage the intestinal tract.

Soft woolly toys are special puppy favorites. They come in a wide variety of cute shapes and sizes; some look like little stuffed animals. Puppies love to shake them up and toss them about or simply carry them around. Be careful of fuzzy toys that have button eyes or noses that your pup could chew off and swallow, and make sure that he does not disembowel a squeaky toy to remove the squeaker! Braided rope toys are similar in that they are fun to chew and toss around, but they shred easily and the strings are easy to swallow. The strings are not digestible and, if the puppy doesn't pass them in his stool, he could end up at the vet's office. Your puppy should be closely monitored with rope toys.

Dandies require toys to chew on as well as toys to sleep with. A nylon rope toy and a nylon bone are two of the safest dog toys available. Visit your pet store to see the wide selection of toys available. Dandies do not destroy toys the way many other dogs do. Some Dandies enjoy soft plush or fleece toys but most want to remove the squeaker as soon as possible, then destuff them and rip up the rest of it. A few Dandies will covet them and they'll last many months as the perfect "crate mate."

Soft latex toys last a while but

Nothing beats a game of fetch!

few Dandies seem to enjoy the hard vinyl toys. Some enjoy the rubber toys and balls, but be sure to buy a large enough ball so that the dog can't accidentally swallow it.

Never give a Dandie rawhide, pig's feet, cow hooves and the like. They leave the coat on the paws and legs a gummy mess, and the Dandie is inclined to swallow pieces which are too large to easily digest.

If you believe that your pup has ingested one of these forbidden objects, check his stools for the next couple of days to see if he passes

GOOD CHEWING

Chew toys run the gamut from rawhide chews to hard sterile bones and everything in between. Rawhides are all-time favorites, but they can cause choking when they become mushy from repeated chewing, causing them to break into small pieces that are easy to swallow. Rawhides are also highly indigestible and should be avoided for the Dandie. Hard sterile bones are great for plaque prevention as well as chewing satisfaction. Dispose of them when the ends become sharp or splintered.

Dandie playtime begins again...

them when he defecates. At the same time, also watch for signs of intestinal distress. A call to your veterinarian might be in order to get his advice and be on the safe side.

Collars

A lightweight nylon collar is the best choice for a very young pup. Quick-click collars are easy to put on and remove, and they can be adjusted as the puppy grows. Introduce him to his collar as soon as he comes home to get him accustomed to wearing it. He'll get used to it quickly and won't mind a bit. Make sure that it is snug enough that it won't slip off, yet loose enough to be comfortable for the pup. You should be able to slip two fingers between the collar and his neck. Check the collar often, as puppies grow in spurts, and his collar can become too tight almost overnight. Choke collars are for training purposes only and should never be used on a puppy under five months old.

Leashes

A 6-foot nylon lead is an excellent choice for a young puppy. It is lightweight and not as tempting to chew as a leather lead. You can switch to a 6-foot leather lead after your pup has grown and is used to walking politely on a lead. For initial puppy walks and house-training purposes, you should invest in a shorter lead so that you have more control over the puppy. At first, you don't want him wandering too far away from you, and when taking him out for toileting you will want to keep him in the specific area chosen for his potty spot.

Once the puppy is heel trained

with a traditional leash, you can consider purchasing a retractable lead. A retractable lead is excellent for walking adult dogs that are already leash-wise. This type of lead allows the dog to roam farther away from you and explore a wider area when out walking, and also retracts when you need to keep him close to you.

HOME SAFETY FOR YOUR PUP

The importance of puppy-proofing cannot be overstated. In addition to making your house comfortable for your Dandie's arrival, you also must make sure that your house is safe for your puppy before you bring him home. There are countless hazards in the owner's personal living environment that a pup can sniff, chew, swallow or destroy. Many are obvious; others are not. Do a thorough advance house check to remove or rearrange those things that could hurt your puppy, keeping any potentially dangerous items out of areas to which he will have access.

Electrical cords are especially dangerous, since puppies view them as irresistible chew toys. Unplug and remove all exposed cords or fasten them beneath a baseboard where the puppy cannot reach them. Veterinarians and firefighters can tell you horror stories about electrical burns and house fires that resulted from puppy-chewed electrical cords. Consider this a most serious precaution for your

TOXIC PLANTS
Plants are natural puppy magnets, but many can be harmful, even fatal, if ingested by a puppy or adult dog. Scout your yard and home interior and remove any plants, bushes or flowers that could be even mildly dangerous. It could save your puppy's life. You can obtain a complete list of toxic plants from your veterinarian, at the public library or by looking online.

puppy and the rest of your family.

Scout your home for tiny objects that might be seen at a pup's eye level. Keep medication bottles and cleaning supplies well out of reach, and do the same with waste baskets and other trash containers. It goes without saying that you should not use rodent poison or other toxic chemicals in any puppy area and

tools are usually kept there. It's best to keep these areas off limits to the pup. Antifreeze is especially dangerous to dogs, as they find the taste appealing and it takes only a few licks from the driveway to kill a dog, puppy or adult, small breed or large.

VISITING THE VETERINARIAN

A good veterinarian is your Dandie puppy's best health-insurance policy. If you do not already have a vet, ask friends and experienced dog people in your area for recommendations so that you can select a vet before you bring your Dandie puppy home. Also arrange for your puppy's first veterinary examination beforehand, since many vets have two- and three-week waiting periods and your puppy should visit the vet within a day or so of coming home.

It's important to make sure your puppy's first visit to the vet is a pleasant and positive one. The vet should take great care to befriend the pup and handle him gently to make their first meeting a positive experience. The vet will give the pup a thorough physical examination and set up a schedule for vaccinations and other necessary wellness visits. Be sure to show your vet any health and inoculation records, which you should have received from your breeder. Your vet is a great source of canine health information, so be sure to ask questions and take notes.

Dandies aren't particular about what they chew or eat, but you'd better be.

that you must keep such containers safely locked up. You will be amazed at how many places a curious puppy can discover!

Once your house has cleared inspection, check your yard. A sturdy fence, well embedded into the ground, will give your dog a safe place to play and potty. Although Dandies are not known to be climbers or fence jumpers, they are still athletic dogs, so a 5-foot fence should suffice to contain an agile youngster or adult. Dandies are rarely climbers. Check the fence periodically for necessary repairs. If there is a weak link or space to squeeze through, you can be sure a determined Dandie will discover it.

The garage and shed can be hazardous places for a pup, as things like fertilizers, chemicals and

ASK THE VET

Help your vet help you to become a well-informed dog owner. Don't be shy about becoming involved in your puppy's veterinary care by asking questions and gaining as much knowledge as you can. For starters, ask what shots your puppy is getting and what diseases they prevent, and discuss with your vet the safest way to vaccinate. Find out what is involved in your dog's annual wellness visits. If you plan to spay or neuter, discuss the best age at which to have this done. Start out on the right "paw" with your puppy's vet and develop good communication with him, as he will care for your dog's health throughout the dog's entire life.

Creating a health journal for your puppy will make a handy reference for his wellness and any future health problems that may arise.

MEETING THE FAMILY

Your Dandie's homecoming is an exciting time for all members of the family, and it's only natural that everyone will be eager to meet him, pet him and play with him. However, for the puppy's sake, it's best to make these initial family meetings as uneventful as possible so that the pup is not overwhelmed with too much too soon. Remember, he has just left his dam and his littermates and is away from the breeder's home for the first time.

Despite his fuzzy wagging tail, he is still apprehensive and wondering where he is and who all these strange humans are. It's best to let him explore on his own and meet the family members as he feels comfortable. Let him investigate all the new smells, sights and sounds at his own pace. Children should be especially careful to not get overly excited, use loud voices or hug the pup too tightly. Be calm, gentle and affectionate, and be ready to comfort him if he appears frightened or uneasy.

Be sure to show your puppy his new crate during this first day home. Toss a treat or two inside the crate; if he associates the crate with food, he will associate the crate with good things. If he is comfortable with the crate, you can offer him his first meal inside it. Leave the door ajar so he can wander in and out as he chooses.

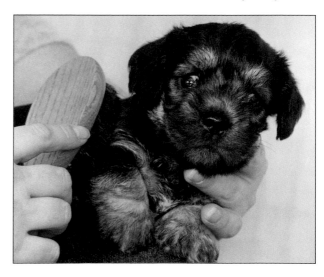

Gentle brushing is a good way to introduce your pup to his future grooming routine.

SOCIALIZING YOUR PUPPY

The first 20 weeks of your Dandie puppy's life are the most important of his entire lifetime. A properly socialized puppy will grow up to be a confident and stable adult who will be a pleasure to live with and a welcome addition to the neighborhood.

The importance of socialization cannot be overemphasized. Research on canine behavior has proven that

"Come, they told me!" Hobergays Drummer Boy, bred by Josie Whittall and owned by Dr. Emma Greenway.

THE FIRST FAMILY MEETING
Your puppy's first day at home should be quiet and uneventful. Despite his wagging tail, he is still wondering where his mom and siblings are! Let him make friends with other members of the family on his own terms; don't overwhelm him. You have a lifetime ahead to get to know each other!

puppies who are not exposed to new sights, sounds, people and animals during their first 20 weeks of life will grow up to be timid and fearful, even aggressive, and unable to flourish outside of their home environment. Dandies should not be released to their homes until 11 or 12 weeks of age.

Socializing your puppy is not difficult and, in fact, will be a fun time for you both. Lead training goes hand in hand with socialization, so your puppy will be learning how to walk on a lead at the same time that he's meeting the neighborhood. Because the Dandie is such a terrific breed, your puppy will enjoy being "the new kid on the block." Take him for short walks to the park and to other dog-friendly places where he will encounter new people, especially children. Puppies automatically recognize children as "little people" and are drawn to play with them. Just make sure that you supervise these meetings and that the children do not get too rough or encourage him to play too hard. An overzealous pup can often nip too hard, frightening the child and in turn making the puppy overly excited. A bad experience in puppyhood can impact a dog for life, so a pup that has a negative experience with a child may grow up to be shy or even aggressive around children.

Take your puppy along on your daily errands. Puppies are natural "people magnets," and most people who see your pup will want to pet him. All of these encounters will help to mold him into a confident adult dog. Likewise, you will soon feel like a confident, responsible

Keep your Dandie puppy's experiences happy and safe.

dog owner, rightly proud of your handsome Dandie.

Often a puppy is coming to his new home at a very impressionable time in his development. The 8-to-11-week-old period, which is also called the "fear period," is a serious imprinting period, and all contact during this time should be gentle and positive. A frightening or negative event could leave a permanent impression that could affect his future behavior if a similar situation arises.

Also make sure that your puppy has received his first and second rounds of vaccinations before you expose him to other dogs or bring him to places that other dogs may frequent. Avoid dog parks and other strange-dog areas until your vet assures you that your puppy is fully immunized and resistant to the diseases that can be passed between

At four weeks of age, this mustard pup is King's Mtn. Bailey.

THE CRITICAL SOCIALIZATION PERIOD

Canine research has shown that a puppy's 8th through 16th week is the most critical learning period of his life. This is when the puppy "learns to learn," a time when he needs positive experiences to build confidence and stability. Puppies who are not exposed to different people and situations outside the home during this period can grow up to be fearful and sometimes aggressive. This is also the best time for puppy lessons, since he has not yet acquired any bad habits that could undermine his ability to learn.

canines. Discuss socialization with your breeder, as some breeders recommend socializing the puppy even before he has received all of his inoculations, depending on how outgoing the puppy may be.

The breeder may use ex-pens and gates to separate his house dogs from the Dandie babies.

LEADER OF THE PUPPY'S PACK

Like other canines, your puppy needs an authority figure, someone he can look up to and regard as the leader of his "pack." His first pack leader was his dam, who taught him to be polite and not chew too hard on her ears or nip at her muzzle. He learned those same lessons from his littermates. If he played too rough, they cried in pain and stopped the game, which sent an important message to the rowdy puppy.

As puppies play together, they are also struggling to determine who will be the boss. Being pack animals, dogs need someone to be in charge. If a litter of puppies remained together beyond puppyhood, one of the pups would emerge as the strongest one, the one who calls the shots.

Once your puppy leaves the pack, he will look intuitively for a new leader. If he does not recognize you as that leader, he will try to assume that position for himself. Of course, it is hard to imagine your adorable Dandie puppy trying to be in charge when he is so small and seemingly helpless. You must remember that these are natural canine instincts. Do not cave in and allow your pup to get the upper "paw"!

Just as socialization is so important during these first 20 weeks, so too is your puppy's early education. He was born without any bad habits. He does not know what is good or bad behavior. If he does things like nipping and digging, it's because he is having fun and doesn't know that humans consider these things as "bad." It's your job to teach him proper puppy manners, and this is the best time to accomplish that—before he has developed bad habits, since it is much more difficult to "unlearn" or correct unacceptable learned behavior than to teach good behavior from the start.

Make sure that all members of the family understand the importance of being consistent when training their new puppy. If you tell the puppy to stay off the sofa and your daughter allows him to cuddle on the couch to watch her favorite television show, your pup will be confused about what he is and is not allowed to do. Have a family conference before your pup comes home so that everyone understands the basic principles of puppy training and the rules you have set forth for the pup, and agrees to follow them.

The old saying that "an ounce of prevention is worth a pound of cure"

A mustard bitch and a pepper dog at six weeks of age, enjoying the good life at the author's King's Mtn.

is especially true when it comes to puppies. It is much easier to prevent inappropriate behavior than it is to change it. It's also easier and less stressful for the pup, since it will keep discipline to a minimum and create a more positive learning environment for him. That, in turn, will also be easier on you!

Here are a few commonsense tips to keep your belongings safe and your puppy out of trouble:

- Keep your closet doors closed and your shoes, socks and other apparel off the floor so your puppy can't get at them.
- Keep a secure lid on the trash container or put the trash where your puppy can't dig into it. He can't damage what he can't reach!
- Supervise your puppy at all times to make sure he is not getting into mischief. If he starts to chew the corner of the rug, you can distract him instantly by tossing a toy for him to fetch. You also will be able to whisk him outside when you notice that he is about to piddle on the carpet. If you can't see your puppy, you can't teach him or correct his behavior.

HAPPY PUPPIES COME RUNNING

Never call your puppy (or adult dog) to come to you and then scold him or discipline him when he gets there. He will make a natural association between coming to you and being scolded, and he will think he was a bad dog for coming to you. He will then be reluctant to come whenever he is called. Always praise your puppy every time he comes to you.

DANDIE DINMONT TERRIER

FEEDING THE DANDIE

PUPPIES

Twelve-week-old Dandie puppies are fed twice a day, and I recommend keeping the Dandie on twice daily feeding all of their lives. Most have hearty appetites and look forward to their meals with enthusiasm.

Dandie puppies and youngsters at least 12 months of age do well on a diet consisting primarily of a good commer-

cial dry kibble containing chicken meal and ground corn and rice flour, amply fortified with vitamins and minerals. Dry foods containing at least 28% protein and 17% fat and a minimum of 4% fiber are good choices for the Dandie youngster. I like to make a stew of sauteed ground beef with cooked vegetables such as tomatoes, carrots, green beans and any other tired vegetables found in my fridge. A spoonful or two of this warmed stew over the dry food ensures each bowl is licked spotlessly clean.

MATURE AND SENIOR DANDIES

For the mature Dandie who lives the good life at home, not stressed by competition or breeding, a dry food with lower protein and fat content is the better choice. I have found a dry food based on ground corn fortified with vitamins and minerals with a protein content of only 21% and fat content of 8% to be a good choice.

Dandies should be kept in lean hard condition and sometimes that means you must feed your dog a leaner diet and perhaps less quantity than you fed him as a growing youngster. There are many different commercial dry foods on the market today to satisfy a variety of needs, some marked for the

---

VARIETY IS THE SPICE

Although dog-food manufacturers contend that dogs don't like variety in their diets, studies show quite the opposite to be true. Dogs would much rather vary their meals than eat the same old chow day in and day out. Dry kibble is no more exciting for a dog than the same bowl of bran flakes would be for you. Fortunately, there are dozens of varieties available on the market, and your dog will likely show preference for certain flavors over others. A word of warning: don't overdo it or you'll develop a fussy eater who only prefers chopped beef fillet and asparagus tips every night.

less active or geriatric dog.

Dandies enjoy a variety of fruits and vegetables, and these make delicious low-calorie snacks. Our Dandies enjoy slices of banana, apple or pear, as well as any number of vegetables they talk me into giving them as I make our dinner. Youngsters seem to have no trouble digesting any of this, but sometimes you must exercise some caution in feeding raw fruits and vegetables to senior canine citizens.

Dandies over the age of seven can have difficulty digesting high-protein diets. If your older Dandie is regularly bringing up a bit of yellow bile, or suffers from bouts of "growly tummy" (where the stomach is making thunderous clouds of loud gurgly noises accompanied by inappetence), a geriatric check-up is recommended. Your veterinarian will probably run a geriatric blood panel to check all his bodily functions and probably recommend a diet much reduced in protein and fat content, a diet much more easily digested.

SUPPLEMENTS

The Dandie is a small dog, and most commercially prepared quality foods contain all the vitamin and mineral supplements necessary for his growth, development and maintenance. Be very cautious about supplementing the Dandie beyond what is found in the food, as it is seldom necessary.

DON'T FORGET THE WATER!

For a dog, it's always time for a drink! Regardless of what type of food he eats, there's no doubt that he needs plenty of water. Fresh cold water, in a clean bowl, should be freely available to your dog at all times. There are special circumstances, such as during puppy housebreaking, when you will want to monitor your pup's water intake so that you will be able to predict when he will need to relieve himself, but water must be available to him nonetheless. Water is essential for hydration and proper body function just as it is in humans.

You will get to know how much your dog typically drinks in a day. Of course, in the heat or if exercising vigorously, he will be more thirsty and will drink more. However, if he begins to drink noticeably more water for no apparent reason, this could signal any of various problems, and you are advised to consult your vet.

Water is the best drink for dogs. Some owners are tempted to give milk from time to time or to moisten dry food with milk, but dogs do not have the enzymes necessary to digest the

An adult Dandie does best on twice-daily feedings of a high-quality kibble—and perhaps homemade extras.

lactose in milk, which is much different from the milk that nursing puppies receive. Therefore stick with clean fresh water to quench your dog's thirst, and always have it readily available to him.

EXERCISING THE DANDIE

The young Dandie enjoys a yard and will romp and play and investigate every corner. An opportunity to get out and stretch and do what he would like on his own should be given to him two or three times a day. Between 12 weeks and 6 or 8 months of age, a short walk on collar and lead through the neighborhood is a good idea. Start out with a short trip around your property and very gradually expand the length of the walk. Remember your Dandie puppy has short legs and a long body to synchronize and he isn't as co-ordinated as a puppy as he will be as an adult. Puppies at around a year of age will enjoy a walk at a brisk pace for 20 to 30 minutes once or twice a day.

Dandies are not a breed to choose if you are looking for a companion while you are running or riding a bicycle or a horse. They were not built for that job, and while a few have the heart to try, it is impractical and not in their best interests. There are a few Dandies who enjoy a long walk at a fast clip, and it'll be obvious very quickly whether your Dandie is one of those who does. Never exercise your Dandie during the heat of the day; let him sleep during this time and go out when it cools off. Heat exhaustion is a very real threat to all dogs.

The Dandie must always be walked on lead. Unless you are totally certain you are many miles away from vehicles, it is not safe to let your Dandie off lead. Should a strange cat or squirrel cross his path, even the most obedient Dandie is gone, and no amount of calling on your part is going to cause him to abandon the noble chase until the game is caught.

GROOMING YOUR DANDIE
By Dr. Emma Greenway

The Dandie is not a "wash and wear" breed. If you don't enjoy brushing, combing, bathing and doing minor trimming on a regular basis, then the Dandie is not for you. For Dandie

---

QUENCHING HIS THIRST

Is your dog drinking more than normal and trying to lap up everything in sight? Excessive drinking has many different causes. Obvious causes for a dog's being thirstier than usual are hot weather and vigorous exercise. However, if your dog is drinking more for no apparent reason, you could have cause for concern. Serious conditions like kidney or liver disease, diabetes and various types of hormonal problems can all be indicated by excessive drinking. If you notice your dog's being excessively thirsty, contact your vet at once. Hopefully there will be a simpler explanation, but the earlier a serious problem is detected, the sooner it can be treated, with a better rate of cure.

devotees, no amount of work detracts from the sheer pleasure of being owned by one of the great characters of the canine world. Trimming your Dandie yourself can be an enormously satisfying task; however, it is not for everyone and many owners opt to have their pet regularly groomed by a professional. When deciding where to take your dog, it is important to remember that this is a rare breed and most groomers don't know how a Dandie should be trimmed.

Once you've selected a groomer, take along photos and drawings of how you want your Dandie to look—or simply this book. This will help the groomer to know exactly what you want. How often you decide to get your Dandie groomed and whether you choose to have him clipped or stripped depends upon your personal taste. Some owners like to have their Dandie in a neat and tidy jacket with trimmed furnishings. This requires the dog to be groomed at a minimum of every six to eight weeks. Other owners like their Dandie to have a more scruffy and shaggy appearance and may only choose to have their dog groomed at the change of every season. Regardless of how often your dog is professionally trimmed, your Dandie will require regular maintenance by you at home.

Whether you're grooming your beloved pet or learning to trim your Dandie for showing, it is immensely easier if you have the proper equipment to do the job right. Here's some of the equipment you should consider owning:

All groomed up and awaiting their turn in the ring.

- grooming table (if you're tall you can also purchase "leg extenders" which will make working at the table much easier on your back)
- grooming arm that attaches to the grooming table, and a noose into which the dog's head and neck are placed (and never leave your dog unattended on a table while in or out of the noose!)
- soft wire slicker brush (for the body coat)
- pin brush (for the topknot)
- medium-tooth metal comb, preferably Teflon® coated
- fine-tooth metal comb
- 2 stripping knives (coarse and fine)
- Mars Coat King™ stripping comb
- white grooming chalk, either loose chalk or a block of chalk
- toenail clippers and styptic powder (to stop any bleeding)
- thinning shears
- straight scissors
- electric barber's clippers with #10 blade and #4 blade
- hair dryer
- large mirror (when grooming for the show ring)

Weekly Pet Maintenance

Once or twice a week brush the coat. Start with the body and tail, using the soft wire slicker brush, always brushing in the direction the coat grows. Brush each leg, being sure to do the armpit of the forelegs where hair tangles the most, and the underbody as well. Then using the medium-tooth comb go through the body, legs and tail, and repeat again using the fine-tooth comb, being sure to comb right down to the skin.

For the head, use the pin brush and brush the topknot in all directions. If there is a mat in the topknot, use the medium-tooth comb and your fingers to carefully work the mat out. Use the wire slicker brush for the beard, and then the medium comb. Dandies are particularly prone to getting knots in their cheeks, so make sure you brush and comb the hair under the ears.

Looking dapper in her show coat, here's Ch. Pennywise Gambit at the Montgomery County show.

Bathing

Always brush and comb your dog, and trim his nails, before bathing him. Dandie puppies often require a bath once a week due to their inherent desire to go to ground and play in the dirt. Adult Dandies usually require a bath every two or three weeks unless they too have been on a hunting expedition and become especially grubby and smelly.

Nails

Once a week trim the toenails. Many Dandie Dinmont Terriers are foot-sensitive and make a big fuss about having their nails clipped back. Ignore the dog's protests; this is a necessary part of grooming for any dog and eventually the dog learns to accept it. As you well know from clipping your own fingernails, it does not hurt!

Cut just outside the pink bloodline visible on light-colored nails; in dark nails, remove only the hook-like part of the nail that turns down. Should you accidentally cut the "quick" (the blood vessel that goes through the center of each nail) and cause the nail to bleed, dab the nail tip with the styptic powder to stop the bleeding.

For those few dogs who make it almost impossible to trim their nails, some owners find success using an electric (or battery-powered) pet nail grinder, which uses a special sandpaper disc and grinds the nails back.

THE DANDIE COAT

The Dandie coat does not shed. The Dandie may bring plenty of dirt and dander into the house, but he does not drop his coat. Mother Nature intended for it to be pulled and, no, it does not hurt him to have his coat plucked. Any Dandie claiming that it hurts is trying to pull the wool over your eyes!

Dandies get their color from the tips of the individual hair shafts. Each dog is different, but generally the color portion of the hair shaft is about a half-inch in length. In order to have a dog who has color to his coat, obviously mustard or pepper, the coat must be pulled out. The new coat coming in gives them their color. As the coat grows longer, the dark color is on the end of the hair shafts, and the rest of the hair shaft is lighter colored, creamy in the mustard dog and silvery in the pepper dog. The coat is a mixture of approximately two-thirds crisp outer coat to approximately one-third soft undercoat. When the coat is approaching the preferred 2 inches in length, it is at that point that the crisp coat will hang in tufts over the shorter lighter colored undercoat, giving the unique "pencilled" appearance the standard describes. A Dandie whose coat has been clippered all over will have little color and will be either creamy colored if he's a mustard or silvery colored if he's a pepper.

Many Dandie fanciers enjoy the time spent grooming their dogs. They find it relaxing and therapeutic, a

time to sit quietly working on the dog, much like some people enjoy knitting, crocheting or woodworking. Plucking and trimming a Dandie well, however, takes time, experience and expertise. It is almost a lost art, so please don't be discouraged if your Dandie does not look as well groomed as those pictured in this book. With time, you'll improve and your Dandie will look like the Dandie he is, and that should be your goal.

The dog's color comes from the dark end of each hair shaft.

PUPPY PLUCKING

Dandie puppies are born very dark colored. The mustards are very dark brown and the peppers are born black and tan. The mustard coat grows out to be varying shades of red, and the pepper coat is a bluish black. By 16 to 18 weeks of age, these dark tips have grown out, leaving several inches of lighter-colored coat showing as well. It is at this point that the puppy coat needs to be pulled off. Do not bathe the puppy and then try to pull his coat, as the slippery clean coat is

much more difficult to grasp and pull than a fairly dirty coat. If more traction is needed, either dip your fingers in white grooming chalk or put on surgical rubber gloves. If the outer coat with the dark tips doesn't pull out easily, then you need to wait another two or three weeks and then it will come out more easily.

Start at the back of the body and with the comb lift up a half-inch of long coat. Use one hand to hold the skin taut against the body and the other hand's thumb and forefinger to grasp and pull a small amount of the coat out. We call this "plucking," much like plucking a chicken of his feathers. The dog will object if you try to pull too large a clump out. Pluck only the longer crisp outer coat. The soft downy undercoat remains in place. Dandies are not "stripped" down to the skin like some of the other terrier breeds—their underwear is left on. Repeat the process over the rear thighs, the top of the tail, up the back, down the sides of the body, up the neck to the point where the skull joins the body up the chest from the breastbone to under the throat. Be sure to leave the coat on either side

of the breastbone, the coat that covers the two indentations, or you'll create the look of a pigeon breast.

It is important to realize this process will take several hours, not minutes, and the puppy may tire of being held still for long periods of time. You may wish to work for a half hour or so and then take a short break; however, if the puppy is cooperative and content, persevere and get the job done while he's being mellow.

When you've finished pulling the body coat, take the coarsest of the stripping knives and begin raking the undercoat with it. You will have to stop many times to pull the soft undercoat from the teeth of the stripping knife. Be careful as you rake along the area of the spine that you don't accidentally cut the skin over the vertebrae. Keep raking as long as plenty of undercoat is coming out. Now use the fine-toothed stripping knife, pulling more and more undercoat out. One more word about the use of stripping knives: never pull the crisp body coat out using only a stripping knife unless you have mastered the technique of holding and using the knife so you don't cut the coat. Cutting the coat will result in its looking patchy and moth-eaten or, as some would say, "having been groomed with a knife and fork!"

After the body coat has been plucked and the whole body raked well with the stripping knives, it's time for a bath, as the head and furnishings need to be clean to be properly trimmed. Bathe the dog, towel him dry and then finish the drying process using a hair dryer, being careful not to have the dryer on "high," as this can easily burn a dog's sensitive skin. Brush the coat in the direction it grows as you dry the coat.

TRIMMING THE FURNISHINGS

Trimming the legs is fairly simple. Brush the leg coat up and out so that as far as possible the hair is standing out and away from the leg; use an egg-beater motion with your brush to best achieve this. When the hair is brushed into position, hold the foot in one hand and with thinning shears trim the longest coat off, attempting to even the leg coat so as to appear like a post, tree trunk or a table leg when you're finished. The forelegs are trimmed from the elbow joint to the foot. You will find that in order to have a smooth transition from the body coat on the shoulder to the leg furnishings you will need to trim the hair on the elbow quite short; as you trim farther down the leg the hair will be longer. With straight scissors trim the long coat off around the outside of the foot.

The rear legs are trimmed from the hock joint to the foot. With straight scissors trim the long coat off around the outside of the foot, leaving it short and tidy, reflecting the foot's round shape. Scissor the long hair off the bottom of each foot, and be sure to trim the long coat from between the pads, which is where small rocks, mats and burs can hide. The furnishings on the front of the (rear) stifles are also trimmed short and follow the line of the thigh muscles.

The underline is trimmed to reflect the topline, shorter under the loin and tapering in a gentle curve down under the chest. On pets this underline is accomplished by using a combination of the thinning shears in the stifle and loin area and plucking with thumb and forefinger under the chest. From the front use thinning shears to trim the furnishings shorter on the chest, in a loose "V" shape.

The tail is trimmed to look like the short curved sword used in olden times called a scimitar. The hair on top of the tail is plucked, while the softer coat under the tail is plucked short into a scimitar shape. If the puppy is not being shown, this shape can be accomplished by using thinning shears.

Using the electric clippers with a #10 size blade, clip the hair off the penis on the male puppy and the area just in front of the penis, which keeps the little boy Dandie cleaner. On the female Dandie use the clippers to take the hair off around her vulva and

Master groomer and breeder Emma Greenway presents six-month-old Jollygaze Time Lord, "Kevin," on the grooming table.

crotch. Be especially careful when trimming around your Dandie's genitals.

TRIMMING THE EARS

The outer ear leather is also plucked from the natural fold of the ear downward. From the fold of the ear upwards the hair is left long and becomes part of the topknot. The tip of the Dandie's ear ends with a thin tassel, the top of the tassel being an inverted "V." The inner ear is trimmed of long hair by using scissors or clippers with the #10 blade, leaving the same tassel shape on the inside of the ear as is on the outside.

For the coat on the cheeks of the skull, where the ear leather hugs the cheeks, trim short either by plucking or by using thinning shears.

Using thumb and forefinger or very carefully with tweezers, pull the hair from the ear canals to keep air flowing freely into the ear canal. Ear problems can result from ear passages that get little circulating air and become moist havens for infections.

TRIMMING THE HEAD

Brush the clean and dried topknot thoroughly with the pin brush. Brush the beard downwards using the slicker brush. The purist method of trimming the bridge of the muzzle is to pull the coat off using thumb and forefinger, or you may opt to use thinning shears to trim this coat off, or a combination of the two. Pull the coat at the stop (that point where the bridge of the muzzle joins the skull between the eyes), and be sure to pull those hairs that point toward the eyes which, if left long and untrimmed, can irritate the eyes and cause excessive watering.

With thinning shears, trim the beard short and trim the tassels to about the same length as the beard. If the beard and tassels are allowed to get really long, they detract from the true expression of the Dandie, giving the dog a droopy and hangdog look.

The texture of the topknot varies from dog to dog. The original Dandie had a truly silky topknot, and the dog was quite mature before he had much topknot. For better or worse, the Dandie today has a topknot which is more profuse, with more texture, some of which border on being cottony. The result may not be entirely proper, but a more profuse topknot is easier to trim. The effect you want is a rounded topknot that crowns the skull and, along with the ears and beard, frames the face.

There are several methods of trimming the topknot. The desired effect is a natural one, not a barbered or caricatured look. The original method used by Dandie Dinmont and his fellow breeders was singeing, burning the tips of the topknot hairs into the desired shape. Only a Dandie Dinmont Terrier, the most trusting breed on the face of the earth, would allow someone to light his topknot afire with a match. We do not recommend Mr. Dinmont's method today. A second method is breaking the hair off by holding a bit of the hair firmly between your fingers and using your other hand to break the longest hairs off. This method may demand more time than even the most devoted owner has to give. The easiest method is to shape the topknot using blunt or dull thinning shears. The topknot is shorter over the forehead and upper area of the ears and back of the skull, and longer on top, the effect being a crowning topknot.

ROLLING THE COAT

The easiest coat to look after is the one that is worked all the time. Brush and comb the coat vigorously, loosening some of the undercoat and longer crisp coat. After the weekly brushing and combing, take another 15 to 30 minutes and go through the body coat, pulling the longest coat out. This keeps the coat

on the short side, and with new coat constantly coming, the result is a coat that is very easy to care for. The use of a Mars Coat King™, which resembles a de-matter, can also assist in weekly coat maintenance in the pet Dandie as it combines both pulling and thinning the coat when used like a comb.

CLIPPING THE COAT

Some Dandie owners do not have the time or inclination to learn to pluck and trim their Dandies. There are few professional groomers who are interested in grooming a Dandie in this time-consuming manner, and even fewer know how. The very few who could do the job competently would properly demand a great deal of money to compensate them for the hours spent,

Here's Harry: Aust. Grand/Am. Ch. Hobergays Fineus Fogg at 18 months of age with Emma Greenway.

Characteristics of the Dandie's head furnishings, as shown by "Kricket," include the crowning topknot, the beard and the tassels, which should be kept about the same length as the beard.

a #10 blade (a full-tooth blade giving a smooth finish). The professional groomer can trim the head and furnishings using a combination of straight scissors and thinning shears. The main drawback is that the dog will not have good color or the desired coat texture that results from the hand method of trimming.

TRIMMING THE SHOW DANDIE

Perhaps the hardest but most important thing a novice dog exhibitor and groomer must do is actually pick up the stripping knife or thinning shears and have a go—that's right, over the years my observation of people new to grooming is that a paralysis of the fingers overtakes them and they break out in a cold sweat when confronted with actually having to remove hair from their dog. The only words of comfort I can give you here is that the most valuable and useful lessons I have learned in grooming have come from grooming a very poor-quality specimen that I had to figure out how to make look better...and from actually making horrendous mistakes. The beauty of hair is that it is very forgiving and it grows back! Actually in having taught a great many people how to groom, the most common mistakes I have observed are that people usually fail to take out enough hair when they start. Less hair often appears more if it is shaped and trimmed correctly. Leg furnishings and topknots in particular often look fuller and thicker when shortened sufficiently. Remember long hair is heavy and will droop.

so the viable alternative is a trim with electric clippers. If this is what you decide, that is fine, as the Dandie can be clippered into the shape of a Dandie and he doesn't have to resemble a Miniature Schnauzer or a Scottish Terrier or a Poodle. How then is this accomplished?

The dog is brushed and combed and then bathed and dried with a hair dryer. Use the electric clippers with a #4 blade (a skip-tooth blade) for the body, which leaves the body coat with a bit of a shaggy look, rather than a coat all one length. This blade is used in the same places where the body coat would be plucked. The ears can be trimmed using

A STEP-BY-STEP GROOMING PROCEDURE
Tackling the Body Coat

Aim: To end up with a coat of correct texture, approximately the correct length, sitting sufficiently flat so as to show off the curvy smooth outline of the dog.

The Dandie jacket is made of a unique mixture of two-thirds crisp outer coat to one-third soft undercoat; it is ideally approximately 2 inches long and sits in "pencils," in other words some undercoat is visible through the top coat, making the Dandie coat visually different than the harsh tight jacket of a Wire Fox Terrier or Miniature Schnauzer. To keep the jacket in show condition it must be stripped or plucked. Stripping can be done either by hand using the finger and thumb or with a stripping knife. Many people are opposed to the use of the stripping knife, but if used correctly I defy anyone to tell the difference between a coat hand plucked or stripped with a knife.

Hand plucking is described in the section on pet grooming and simply involves the pulling of the crisp hair and then the raking out of undercoat. This raking can be done by dragging a fine-toothed stripping knife through the soft undercoat in the direction that the hair grows.

Using a stripping knife requires practice. Essentially the stripping knife is grasped in the hand and the hair is caught between the knife and your thumb. You then exert a pulling action in the direction that the hair grows. It's most important to remember to keep the knife at right angles to the hair and not to twist the knife when you catch and pull the hair, as this will cut the hair and not pull it.

The area of the Dandie to be stripped consists of the neck from behind the ears and occiput, the throat from Adam's apple to prosternum and then in an inverted "V" to the top of the leg, the body to just below the elbow, following the line of the rib cage into the loin and then down, following the muscle of the thighs to about an inch above the hocks.

The jacket is blended into the areas where furnishings are left on the lower side of the body and on the front of the rear legs by pulling selectively so as to achieve a blended transition. Blending and a natural appearance are key to a correctly presented Dandie in the ring.

The pale hair around the anus is not pulled but shortened with thinning shears; it is never clipped or trimmed so short as to appear clipped. It should

Sandra Pretari, grooming a mustard bitch for the show ring.

Winning under the author, Ch. Schooner Bizzy Weekend Warrior, handled by Donna Johnston for owner Linda Winfrey.

is to evenly pull a little of both top and undercoat out each week while maintaining the jacket in show condition. Taking out about one of every ten crisp hairs each week will achieve this goal. By doing this regularly over a course of about 12 to 14 weeks you will end up with a layered coat that can be kept in condition 12 months of the year.

The additional advantage of this method of maintenance is that, using a mirror to examine your dog's outline as the judge would see it from afar, you can take out extra hair and smooth out any lumps and bumps in the topline or over the shoulders that may be caused by the hair growing more thickly in one place than another. Maintaining the outline should be done each week as part of the rolling coat procedure.

be shortened in such a way as to appear that it has grown and remained at the length to which it has been trimmed.

If you are going to fully strip your Dandie with the intention of showing him you need to strip the coat out at least 12 to 16 weeks beforehand, depending on how quickly your dog's coat grows.

One disadvantage of stripping your dog in one sitting is that the coat comes in at all one length; this makes smoothing out bumps in the topline difficult without making holes in the coat. The other disadvantage is that the coat very quickly becomes "blown," which is sometimes called "blousy," i.e., it gets too long and messy and you then have no alternative but to strip it back and start all over again.

The advantage of rolling the coat is it allows your Dandie to be in show coat all year 'round. The technique of "rolling the coat" can be applied to the general action of stripping or plucking. This involves the weekly pulling of both crisp top coat and undercoat. Your aim

Head

Topknot The Dandie head is large but not out of proportion with the body. For this reason when trimming the Dandie's magnificent halo, or topknot of hair, the amount you take off should be carefully considered. Leaving too much on can lead to it flopping over the eyes or, if over-shaped and made to be as "boofy" as possible like a Bichon, especially when trimmed with hard scissors, it can lead the Dandie to look like a cartoon character. This is not correct. Never use hard scissors, whether curved or straight, to trim the Dandie topknot. Either break the hair or use thinning shears. There is some disparity between the way the Dandie head is trimmed in the UK, where it is left longer and wispier, and in America, where it tends to be trimmed much more into a distinctive halo shape. Whatever the style, it should best complement the dog's head and have a soft appearance.

Where the topknot meets the beard the hair should be shortened slightly so as to denote a transition from topknot to beard, but there should not be a distinct line. The standard merely describes the topknot as not being confined to the head, it does not even mention the beard explicitly. The hair on the top part of the ear, from the level of the corner of the eye to the skull, is left long and curves to join the topknot. It is shortened by scissoring to become part of the topknot. The hair on the dog's neck, under the ear, is cleaned out to allow the ear to sit cleanly against the side of the head.

Muzzle The top of the muzzle from nose leather to the corner of the eyes is shortened with thinning shears so as to give the appearance that it grows that way. The original Dandies who hunted with the gypsies and tinkers broke their muzzle hair off by constant digging and going to ground. It should never be clippered or scissored to be so short as to look barbered, and there should be no visible scissor marks to show where it has been shortened. The line between this shorter hair and the rest of the beard should be subtly blended.

The beard should be shortened using thinning shears and will be longer at the front than at the throat. This enhances the impression of a strong jaw and muzzle and also allows for the strength and length of neck to be apparent. A long beard will drag the face and expression down and give the appearance that the dog is long in muzzle and short of neck. A good guide to how long the beard should be is to keep it about the same length as the topknot. This will give balance to the head.

Ears Ears should be stripped leaving a tassel at the tip that begins about 1 to 2 inches from the tip and is an inverted "V." The tassel length should match the length of the beard and flow smoothly into the line of the beard so as to become part of the overall head shape. The underside of the ear is clippered, leaving the hair present where it is part of the topknot and the tassel. If your dog has a lot of hair in its ear canals, this should be plucked out on a regular basis.

Eyes The Dandie's eyes are one of his most beautiful features. The dark pigment that frames them is a distinctive feature of the breed. To enhance the round and wise expression, the eyelashes of the Dandie are plucked out carefully to expose the dark pigment. A small amount of hair can be removed from below the eye as well, being careful not to take out so much as to make the dog look as if its eyes are out of proportion and clown-like.

Forechest or Bib
The bib is the hair that is left long over the prosternum. It starts from the

The correct grooming for the inside of the ear leather.

The correct grooming for the exterior of the ear leather. Notice how the feather is about the length of the beard.

prosternum and comes down in an inverted "V" to just inside of the front legs. It is there to protect the dog and in the show ring is used to enhance the strength and power of the forechest. Again the amount of hair you leave on, which should be shaped at its bottom between the legs in a loose "V" shape, should not be so much that it makes the dog look loaded in front. Obviously if your dog is lacking forechest you may choose to leave more hair on, whereas on a well-made dog this bib can be thinned out and shortened using thinning shears and judicious pulling.

Trimming Leg Furnishings

Front Legs I sometimes think there is an overemphasis on hair when it comes to leg furnishings, and most novice groomers, in their anxiety to have enough coat, tend to leave too much hair on the legs, thinking more is better. It is not. The Dandie's legs do have a covering of soft furnishings and they should be trimmed to give the legs a "tree trunk" or pillar-like appearance, which fits with the standard's description of the legs being "short and strong." Careful attention should be given to trimming the hair on the legs short at the elbow so that there is a smooth transition from shoulder to leg and not the impression that the elbows are sticking out well away from the body. Thinning shears should be used for all trimming so as to create a natural appearance. Hair should be brushed up and out in an egg-beater action that leaves the hair separated and sticking straight out. A little chalk can be added to the hair to give it more body if necessary. Brushing can be done with a comb or brush, whichever feels more comfortable to you. Stand in front of the dog and, holding the dog's front paw and raising the leg toward you, trim from elbow to outer foot to create the appearance of a straight line. Do the same on the inside of the leg. You will find because the dog does not have straight bones in its legs that in some places the hair you have left on the leg will be very short while in other places it will be longer. Coming to the side of the dog, now trim from the elbow to the floor so as to create a straight line and do the same from the front of the leg at the elbow to the floor. The feet of a Dandie should be trimmed as a part of the leg rather than as a separate entity. Dandies are digging terriers; their front feet are large and tend to have a slight outward turn. While this is perfectly acceptable, many judges are unaccustomed to this being correct and for this reason the feet should be trimmed to minimize any appearance of outward turn. The hair between the pads should be shortened, but be careful not to trim the hair from behind the pad, as this should be trimmed to form part of the "tree trunk" and when removed can make the dog look down in the pastern.

Hind Legs In much the same way as the front legs should be "tree trunks," so too should the back legs resemble strong and sturdy legs, though the rear feet are smaller. Furnishings on the front of the first and second thigh should be shortened to accentuate the turn of stifle and, if too much is left on, you will give the look of cowboy chaps from behind, and from the side you will make your dog appear shorter in length of body than he is. The transition from crisp dark body coat to soft pale furnishings should never form too distinct a line, but should be subtle and blended as if it has just grown that way and merely been tidied into shape.

The hock furnishings should be shortened so they are light enough in weight to be brushed up and out. If there is too much hair, the hair will droop and it will be harder to create the sturdy look to the legs. Leaving a little more hair on the rear of the hocks and particularly at the back of the rear pads, the trimming from hock to ground to give an appearance of a straight line will accentuate the dog's turn of stifle and avoid the dog's appearing sickle-hocked.

Underbelly and Underline Trimming
Using a combination of pulling by hand and using thinning shears, the underline of the dog should be shaped to complement the topline. There should be no straight hard lines in the grooming of the topline or underline of a Dandie, and creating them will make your dog appear to lack depth of chest and will create the illusion that the dog is lacking a curvy topline. Again the transition from crisp body coat to the softer furnishings on the underside of the dog should be subtle, be blended and never be a straight hard line. When trimming the underline, ensure that the highest point is at the loin and that there is a gentle curve to the underline as it flows to and along the brisket. Too sharp a tuck-up can make a dog look shorter than it is, as well as make the dog look overly heavy in front and out of balance with his rear. Never forget that the Dandie Dinmont Terrier is an agile and athletic dog, able to twist and turn; he should not ever appear heavy and cumbersome. Resist the temptation to leave profuse furnishings on the underneath just because you have them; they serve no working purpose and if your Dandie Dinmont Terrier has the correct depth of chest there will be no need for them.

Trimming the Tail

The top part of the tail is stripped, either by hand or stripping knife, to accentuate the tail as a continuation of the curvy topline, coming just off the slightly sloping croup. The underside has softer and paler hair, and this is pulled back to accentuate the scimitar shape of a correct tail. This underside hair should never be left so long as to be like the tail of a setter; there is no functional use for such hair in a working Dandie, and it is unnecessary.

THE DAY BEFORE AND DAY OF THE SHOW

Ensure that your dog's jacket is in good clean condition by brushing it thoroughly and taking out any hair that is sticking up and changing the outline of the dog. Do not wash the dog's jacket right before a show, as you will soften it and it will stick up everywhere, since bathing removes the natural oils from the coat. If you wish to wash the dog's jacket, do so at least five days before the show. With regular brushing, a dog's jacket should stay clean and healthy for many weeks. Wash the leg furnishings, beard and topknot only; put some chalk or talcum into the furnishings and topknot and brush thoroughly. When all the hair is in position, sticking up and out, re-trim any hair that may be detracting from the overall outline you are trying to achieve. You will be amazed at how a small amount of hair can be made to look thick and profuse.

FOOD FOR THOUGHT

This outline is by no means a comprehensive description of grooming the Dandie for the show ring. It is only a beginning. One way to begin to understand the standard and to become a better groomer is to collect photos and articles about the breed. Watch other people groom their dogs; observe their techniques and how they use their equipment; and ask questions of them as to why they are doing things in a particular way. Begin to decide what you like and don't like about how various dogs are presented and always be mindful of whether the trim complements the dog, making him appear more like the ideal or whether the dog's trim enhances a fault or even creates a fault in the dog that actually isn't there. Grooming can make a dog look better than he is, but a poor understanding of the dog and the standard can also lead to a dog's being groomed to look worse than he is, often for the sake of leaving on seemingly glamorous amounts of hair. Bear in mind that the standard is a written template and is open to a degree of interpretation. In doing all of this what you are beginning to do is develop your own personal interpretation of the standard, your aim being to imprint upon your mind a template of the perfect Dandie Dinmont Terrier. It is this template that is what you must strive to achieve by your grooming and, if you are a breeder also, by your careful selection of breeding stock.

HOUSE-TRAINING YOUR DANDIE DINMONT TERRIER

Dogs are "touch sensitive" when it comes to house-training. In other words, they respond to the surface on which they are given approval to eliminate. The choice is yours (the dog's version is in parentheses): The lawn (including the neighbors' lawns)? A bare patch of earth under a tree (where people like to sit and relax in the summertime)? Concrete steps or patio (all sidewalks, garages and basement floors)? The curbside (watch out for cars)? A small area of crushed stone in a corner of the yard (mine!)? The latter is the best choice if you can manage it, because it will remain strictly for the dog's use and is easy to keep clean.

You can start out with paper-training indoors and switch over to an outdoor surface as the puppy matures and gains control over his need to eliminate. For the naysayers, don't worry—this won't mean that the dog will soil on every piece of newspaper lying around the house. You are training him to go outside, remember? Starting out by paper-training often is the only choice for a city dog.

When Your Puppy's "Got to Go"

Your puppy's need to relieve himself is seemingly non-stop, but signs of improvement will be seen each week. From 8 to 10 weeks old, the puppy will have to be taken outside every time he wakes up, about 10-15 minutes after every meal and after every period of play—all day long, from first thing in the morning until his bedtime! That's a total of ten or more trips per day to teach the puppy where it's okay to relieve himself. With that schedule in mind, you can see that house-training a young puppy is not a part-time job. It requires someone to be home all day.

If that seems overwhelming or impossible, do a little planning. For example, plan to pick up your puppy at the start of a vacation period. If you can't get home in the middle of the

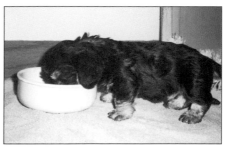

At five weeks of age, this puppy is being weaned.

enchanted by the smell of your cooking (and will never be critical when you burn something). An exercise pen (also called an "ex-pen," a puppy version of a playpen) within the room of choice is an excellent means of confinement for a young pup. He can see out and has a certain amount of space in which to run about, but he is safe from dangerous things like electrical cords, heating units, trash baskets or open kitchen-supply cabinets. Place the pen where the puppy will not get a blast of heat or air conditioning.

In the pen, you can put a few toys, his bed (which can be his crate if the dimensions of pen and crate are compatible) and a few layers of newspaper in one small corner, just in

Although an occasional reprimand may be necessary, training your Dandie is not about scolding him. Instead, it is about setting the rules so you can enjoy each other's company to the fullest.

day, plan to hire a dog-sitter or ask a neighbor to come over to take the pup outside, feed him his lunch and then take him out again about ten or so minutes after he's eaten. Also make arrangements with that or another person to be your "emergency" contact if you have to stay late on the job. Remind yourself—repeatedly—that this hectic schedule improves as the puppy gets older.

HOME WITHIN A HOME

Your Dandie Dinmont Terrier puppy needs to be confined to one secure, puppy-proof area when no one is able to watch his every move. Generally, the kitchen is the place of choice because the floor is washable. Likewise, it's a busy family area that will accustom the pup to a variety of noises, everything from pots and pans to the telephone, blender and dishwasher. He will also be

DAILY SCHEDULE

How many relief trips does your puppy need per day? A puppy up to the age of 14 weeks will need to go outside about 8 to 12 times per day! You will have to take the pup out any time he starts sniffing around the floor or turning in small circles, as well as after naps, meals, games and lessons or whenever he's released from his crate. Once the puppy is 14 to 22 weeks of age, he will require only 6 to 8 relief trips. At the ages of 22 to 32 weeks, the puppy will require about 5 to 7 trips. Adult dogs typically require 4 relief trips per day, in the morning, afternoon, evening and late at night.

case. A water bowl can be hung at a convenient height on the side of the ex-pen so it won't become a splashing pool for an innovative puppy. His food dish can go on the floor, near but not under the water bowl.

Crates are something that pet owners are at last getting used to for their dogs. Wild or domestic canines have always preferred to sleep in den-like safe spots, and that is exactly what the crate provides. How often have you seen adult dogs that choose to sleep under a table or chair even though they have full run of the house? It's the den connection.

In your "happy" voice, use the word "Crate" every time you put the pup into his den. If he's new to a crate, toss in a small biscuit for him to chase the first few times. At night, after he's been outside, he should sleep in his crate. The crate may be kept in his designated area at night or, if you want to be sure to hear those wake-up yips in the morning, put the crate in a corner of your bedroom. However, don't make any response whatsoever to whining or crying. If he's completely ignored, he'll settle down and get to sleep.

Good bedding for a young puppy is an old folded bath towel or an old blanket, something that is easily washable and disposable if necessary ("accidents" will happen!). Never put newspaper in the puppy's crate. Also those old ideas about adding a clock to replace his mother's heartbeat, or a hot-water bottle to replace her warmth, are just that—old ideas. The clock could drive the puppy nuts, and the hot-water bottle could end up as a very soggy waterbed! An extremely good breeder would have introduced your puppy to the crate by letting two pups sleep together for a couple of nights, followed by several nights alone. How thankful you will be if you found that breeder!

Safe toys in the pup's crate or area will keep him occupied, but monitor their condition closely. Discard any toys that show signs of being chewed to bits. Squeaky parts, bits of stuffing or plastic or any other small pieces can cause intestinal blockage or possibly choking if swallowed.

PROGRESSING WITH POTTY-TRAINING

After you've taken your puppy out and he has relieved himself in the area you've selected, he can have some free time with the family as long as there is someone responsible for watching him. That doesn't mean just someone in the same room who is watching TV or busy on the computer, but one person who is doing nothing other than keeping an eye on the pup,

Male dogs lift their leg to urinate whereas females squat. Regardless of sex, your Dandie will pick a favorite spot for its relief area.

Crate training is a bore to this little fellow.

playing with him on the floor and helping him understand his position in the pack.

This first taste of freedom will let you begin to set the house rules. If you don't want the dog on the furniture, now is the time to prevent his first attempts to jump up onto the couch. The word to use in this case is "Off," not "Down." "Down" is the word you will use to teach the down position, which is something entirely different.

Most corrections at this stage come in the form of simply distracting the puppy. Instead of telling him "No" for "Don't chew the carpet," distract the chomping puppy with a toy and he'll forget about the carpet.

As you are playing with the pup, do not forget to watch him closely and pay attention to his body language. Whenever you see him begin to circle or sniff, take the puppy outside to relieve himself. If you are paper-training, put him back into his confined area on the newspapers. In either case, praise him as he eliminates while he actually is in the act of relieving himself. Three seconds after he has finished is too late! You'll be praising him for running toward you, picking up a toy or whatever he may be doing at that moment, and that's not what you want to be praising him for. Timing is a vital tool in all dog training. Use it.

Remove soiled newspapers immediately and replace them with clean ones. You may want to take a small piece of soiled paper and place it in the middle of the new clean papers, as the scent will attract him to that spot when it's time to go again. That scent attraction is why it's so important to clean up any messes made in the house by using a product specially made to eliminate the odor of dog urine and droppings. Regular household cleansers won't do the trick. Pet shops sell the best pet deodorizers. Invest in the largest container you can find.

Scent attraction eventually will lead your pup to his chosen spot outdoors; this is the basis of outdoor training. When you take your puppy outside to relieve himself, use a one-word command such as "Outside" or "Go-potty" (that's one word to the puppy!) as you attach his leash. Then snap the leash on quickly and lead him to his spot. Now comes the hard part—hard for you, that is. Just stand there until he urinates and defecates.

Move him a few feet in one direction or another if he's just sitting there looking at you, but remember that this is neither playtime nor time for a walk. This is strictly a business trip! Then, as he circles and squats (remember your timing!), give him a quiet "Good dog" as praise. If you start to jump for joy, ecstatic over his performance, he'll do one of two things: either he will stop mid-stream, as it were, or he'll do it again for you—in the house—and expect you to be just as delighted.

Give him five minutes or so and, if he doesn't go in that time, take him back indoors to his confined area and try again in another ten minutes, or immediately if you see him sniffing and circling. By careful observation, you'll soon work out a successful schedule.

Accidents, by the way, are just that—accidents. Clean them up quickly and thoroughly, without comment, after the puppy has been taken outside to finish his business and then put back into his area or crate. If you witness an accident in progress, say "No!" in a stern voice and get the pup outdoors immediately. No punishment is needed. You and your puppy are just learning each other's language, and sometimes it's easy to miss a puppy's message. Chalk it up to experience and watch more closely from now on.

KEEPING THE PACK ORDERLY

Discipline is a form of training that brings order to life. For example,

military discipline is what allows the soldiers in an army to work as one. Discipline is a form of teaching and, in dogs, is the basis of how the successful pack operates. Each member knows his place in the pack and all respect the leader, or alpha dog. It is essential for your puppy that you establish this type of relationship, with you as the alpha, or leader. It is a

KIDS RULE

Children of 10 to 12 year of age are old enough to understand the "be kind to dumb animals" approach and will have fun training their dogs, especially to do tricks. It teaches them to be tolerant, patient and appreciative as well as to accept failure to some extent. Young children can be tyrants, making unreasonable demands of the dog and unable to cope with defeat, blaming it all on the dog. Toddlers need not apply.

The earliest training begins within the litter as the pups teach each other the "rules of the pack" through their interactions.

form of social coexistence that all canines recognize and accept. Discipline, therefore, is never to be confused with punishment. When you teach your puppy how you want him to behave, and he behaves properly and you praise him for it, you are disciplining him with a form of positive reinforcement.

For a dog, rewards come in the form of praise, a smile, a cheerful tone of voice, a few friendly pats or a rub of the ears. Rewards are also small food treats. Obviously, that does not mean bits of regular dog food. Instead, treats are very small bits of special things like cheese or pieces of soft dog treats. The idea is to reward the dog with something very small that he can taste and swallow, providing instant positive reinforcement. If he has to take time to chew the treat, by the time he is finished he will have forgotten what he did to earn it.

Your puppy should never be physically punished. The displeasure

shown on your face and in your voice is sufficient to signal to the pup that he has done something wrong. He wants to please everyone higher up on the social ladder, especially his leader, so a scowl and harsh voice will take care of the error. Growling out the word "Shame!" when the pup is caught in the act of doing something wrong is better than the repetitive "No." Some dogs hear "No" so often that they begin to think it's their name! By the way, do not use the dog's name when you're correcting him. His name is reserved to get his attention for something pleasant about to take place.

There are punishments that have nothing to do with you. For example, your dog may think that chasing cats is one reason for his existence. You can try to stop it as much as you like but without success, because it's such fun for the dog. But one good hissing, spitting swipe of a cat's claws across the dog's nose will put an end to the game forever. Intervene only when your dog's eyeball is seriously at risk. Cat scratches can cause permanent damage to an innocent but annoying puppy.

PUPPY KINDERGARTEN

COLLAR AND LEASH
Before you begin your Dandie Dinmont Terrier puppy's education, he must be used to his collar and leash. Choose a collar for your puppy that is secure, but not heavy or bulky. He won't enjoy training if he's

uncomfortable. A flat buckle collar is fine for everyday wear and for initial puppy training. For older dogs, there are several types of training collars such as the martingale, which is a double loop that tightens slightly around the neck, and the head collar, which is similar to a horse's halter. Do not use a chain choke collar unless you have been specifically shown how to put it on and how to use it. You may not be disposed to use a chain choke collar even if your breeder has told you that it's suitable for your Dandie Dinmont Terrier.

A lightweight 6-foot woven cotton or nylon training leash is preferred by most trainers because it is easy to fold up in your hand and comfortable to hold because there is a certain amount of give to it. There are lessons where the dog will start off 6 feet away from you at the end of the leash. The leash used to take the puppy outside to relieve himself is shorter because you don't want him to roam away from his area. The shorter leash will also be the one to use when you walk the puppy.

If you've been wise enough to enroll in a puppy kindergarten training class, suggestions will be made as to the best collar and leash for your young puppy. I say "wise" because your puppy will be in a class with puppies in his age range (up to five months old) of all breeds and sizes. It's the perfect way for him to learn the right way (and the wrong way) to interact with other dogs as well as their people. You cannot teach

LEASH TRAINING

House-training and leash training go hand in hand, literally. When taking your puppy outside to do his business, lead him there on his leash. Unless an emergency potty run is called for, do not whisk the puppy up into your arms and take him outside. If you have a fenced yard, you have the advantage of letting the puppy loose to go out, but it's better to put the dog on the leash and take him to his designated place in the yard until he is reliably house-trained. Taking the puppy for a walk is the best way to house-train a dog. The dog will associate the walk with his time to relieve himself, and the exercise of walking stimulates the dog's bowels and bladder. Dogs that are not trained to relieve themselves on a walk may hold it until they get back home, which of course defeats half the purpose of the walk.

TAPERING OFF TIDBITS

Your dog has been watching you—and the hand that treats—throughout all of his lessons, and now it's time to break the treat habit. Begin by giving him treats at the end of each lesson only. Then start to give a treat after the end of only some of the lessons. At the end of every lesson, as well as during the lessons, be consistent with the praise. Your pup now doesn't know whether he'll get a treat or not, but he should keep performing well just in case! Finally, you will stop giving treat rewards entirely. Save them for something brand-new that you want to teach him. Keep up the praise and you'll always have a "good dog."

your puppy how to interpret another dog's sign language. For a first-time puppy owner, these socialization classes are invaluable. For experienced dog owners, they are a real boon to further training.

ATTENTION

You've been using the dog's name since the minute you collected him from the breeder, so you should be able to get his attention by saying his name—with a big smile and in an excited tone of voice. His response will be the puppy equivalent of "Here I am! What are we going to do?" Your

immediate response (if you haven't guessed by now) is "Good dog." Rewarding him at the moment he pays attention to you teaches him the proper way to respond when he hears his name.

EXERCISES FOR A BASIC CANINE EDUCATION

THE SIT EXERCISE

There are several ways to teach the puppy to sit. The first one is to catch him whenever he is about to sit and, as his backside nears the floor, say "Sit, good dog!" That's positive reinforcement and, if your timing is sharp, he will learn that what he's doing at that second is connected to your saying "Sit" and that you think he's clever for doing it!

Another method is to start with the puppy on his leash in front of you. Show him a treat in the palm of your right hand. Bring your hand up under his nose and, almost in slow motion, move your hand up and back so his nose goes up in the air and his head tilts back as he follows the treat in your hand. At that point, he will have to either sit or fall over, so as his back legs buckle under, say "Sit, good dog," and then give him the treat and lots of praise. You may have to begin with your hand lightly running up his chest, actually lifting his chin up until he sits. Some (usually older) dogs require gentle pressure on their hindquarters with the left hand, in which case the dog should be on your left side. Puppies generally do not appreciate this physical dominance.

After a few times, you should be able to show the dog a treat in the open palm of your hand, raise your hand waist-high as you say "Sit" and have him sit. You thereby will have taught him two things at the same time. Both the verbal command and the motion of the hand are signals for the sit. Your puppy is watching you almost more than he is listening to you, so what you do is just as important as what you say.

Don't save any of these drills only for training sessions. Use them as much as possible at odd times during a normal day. The dog should always sit before being given his food dish. He should sit to let you go through a doorway first, when the doorbell rings or when you stop to speak to someone on the street.

THE DOWN EXERCISE
Before beginning to teach the down command, you must consider how the dog feels about this exercise. To him, "down" is a submissive position. Being flat on the floor with you standing over him is not his idea of fun. It's up to you to let him know that, while it may not be fun, the reward of your approval is worth his effort.

Start with the puppy on your left side in a sit position. Hold the leash right above his collar in your left hand. Have an extra-special treat, such as a small piece of cooked chicken or hot dog, in your right hand. Place it at the end of the pup's

> ### A SIMPLE "SIT"
> When you command your dog to sit, use the word "Sit." Do not say "Sit down," as your dog will not know whether you mean "Sit" or "Down," or maybe you mean both. Be clear in your instructions to your dog; use one-word commands and always be consistent.

nose and steadily move your hand down and forward along the ground. Hold the leash to prevent a sudden lunge for the food. As the puppy goes into the down position, say "Down" very gently.

The difficulty with this exercise is twofold: it's both the submissive aspect and the fact that most people say the word "Down" as if they were drill sergeants in charge of recruits! So issue the command sweetly, give him the treat and have the pup maintain the down position for several seconds. If he tries to get up immediately, place your hands on his shoulders and press down gently, giving him a very quiet "Good dog."

A daughter of Ch. Utzmoor King's Mtn. Edition at four months of age, bred and owned by Mr. and Mrs. Fran LeHoty.

As you progress with this lesson, increase the "down time" until he will hold it until you say "Okay" (his cue for release). Practice this one in the house at various times throughout the day.

By increasing the length of time during which the dog must maintain the down position, you'll find many uses for it. For example, he can lie at your feet in the vet's office or anywhere that both of you have to wait, when you are on the phone, while the family is eating and so forth. If you progress to training for competitive obedience, he'll already be all set for the exercise called the "long down."

THE STAY EXERCISE

You can teach your Dandie Dinmont Terrier to stay in the sit, down and stand positions. To teach the sit/stay, have the dog sit on your left side. Hold the leash at waist level in your left hand and let the dog know that you have a treat in your closed right hand. Step forward on your right foot as you say "Stay." Immediately turn and stand directly in front of the dog, keeping your right hand up high so he'll keep his eye on the treat hand and maintain the sit position for a count of five. Return to your original position and offer the reward.

Increase the length of the sit/stay each time until the dog can hold it for at least 30 seconds without moving. After about a week of success, move out on your right foot and take two steps before turning to face the dog. Give the "Stay" hand signal (left palm back toward the dog's head) as you leave. He gets the treat when you return and he holds the sit/stay. Increase the distance that you walk away from him before turning until you reach the length of your training leash. But don't rush it! Go back to the beginning if he moves before he should. No matter what the lesson, never be upset by having to back up for a few days. The repetition and practice are what will make your dog reliable in these commands. It won't do any good to move on to something more difficult if the command is not mastered at the easier levels. Above all, even if you do get frustrated, never let your puppy know. Always keep a positive, upbeat attitude during training, which will transmit to your dog for positive results.

The down/stay is taught in the same way once the dog is completely reliable and steady with the down command. Again, don't rush it. With

The down exercise may present more of a challenge than the sit, as the dog may feel uncomfortable assuming the down position.

the dog in the down position on your left side, step out on your right foot as you say "Stay." Return by walking around in back of the dog and into your original position. While you are training, it's okay to murmur something like "Hold on" to encourage him to stay put. When the dog will stay without moving when you are at a distance of 3 or 4 feet, begin to increase the length of time before you return. Be sure he holds the down on your return until you say "Okay." At that point, he gets his treat—just so he'll remember for next time that it's not over until it's over.

THE COME EXERCISE

No command is more important to the safety of your Dandie Dinmont Terrier than "Come." It is what you should say every single time you see the puppy running toward you: "Wally, come! Good dog." During playtime, run a few feet away from the puppy and turn and tell him to "Come" as he is already running to you. You can go so far as to teach your puppy two things at once if you squat down and hold out your arms. As the pup gets close to you and you're saying "Good dog," bring your right arm in about waist high. Now he's also learning the hand signal, an excellent device should you be on the phone when you need to get him to come to you! You'll also both be one step ahead when you enter obedience classes.

When the puppy responds to your well-timed "Come," try it with the puppy on the training leash. This

DOWN

"Down" is a harsh-sounding word and a submissive posture in dog body language, thus presenting two obstacles in teaching the down command. When the dog is about to flop down on his own, tell him "Good down." Pups that are not good about being handled learn better by having food lowered in front of them. A dog that trusts you can be gently guided into position. When you give the command "Down," be sure to say it sweetly!

time, catch him off guard, while he's sniffing a leaf or watching a bird: "Wally, come!" You may have to pause for a split second after his name to be sure you have his attention. If the puppy shows any sign of confusion, give the leash a mild jerk and take a couple of steps backward. Do not repeat the command. In this case, you should say "Good come" as he reaches you.

That's the number-one rule of

If you make teaching the come command fun, your dog will always be so happy to see you that he'll come running whenever you call him!

training. Each command word is given just once. Anything more is nagging. You'll also notice that all commands are one word only. Even when they are actually two words, you say them as one.

Never call the dog to come to you—with or without his name—if you are angry or intend to correct him for some misbehavior. When correcting the pup, you go to him. Your dog must always connect "Come" with something pleasant and with your approval; then you can rely on his response.

Puppies, like children, have notoriously short attention spans, so don't overdo it with any of the training. Keep each lesson short. Break it up with a quick run around the yard or a ball toss, repeat the lesson and quit as soon as the pup gets it right. That way, you will always end with a "Good dog."

Life isn't perfect and neither are puppies. A time will come, often around ten months of age, when he'll become "selectively deaf" or choose to "forget" his name. He may respond by wagging his tail (and even seeming to smile at you) with a look that says "Make me!" Laugh, throw his favorite toy and skip the lesson you had planned. Pups will be pups!

THE HEEL EXERCISE
The second most important command to teach, after the come, is the heel. When you are walking your growing puppy, you need to be in control. Besides, it looks terrible to be pulled and yanked down the street, and it's not much fun either. Your 10- to 11-week-old puppy will probably follow you everywhere, but that's his natural instinct, not your control over the situation. However, any time he does follow you, you can say "Heel" and be ahead of the game, as he will learn to associate this command with the

action of following you before you even begin teaching him to heel.

There is a very precise, almost military, procedure for teaching your dog to heel. As with all other obedience training, begin with the dog on your left side. He will be in a very nice sit and you will have the training leash across your chest. Hold the loop and folded leash in your right hand. Pick up the slack leash above the dog in your left hand and hold it loosely at your side. Step out on your left foot as you say "Heel." If the puppy does not move, give a gentle tug or pat your left leg to get him started. If he surges ahead of you, stop and pull him back gently until he is at your side. Tell him to sit and begin again.

Walk a few steps and stop while the puppy is correctly beside you. Tell him to sit and give mild verbal praise. (More enthusiastic praise will encourage him to think the lesson is over.) Repeat the lesson, increasing the number of steps you take only as long as the dog is heeling nicely beside you. When you end the lesson, have him hold the sit, then give him the "Okay" to let him know that this is the end of the lesson. Praise him so that he knows he did a good job.

The cure for excessive pulling (a common problem) is to stop when the dog is no more than 2 or 3 feet ahead of you. Guide him back into position and begin again. With a really determined puller, try switching to a head collar. This will automatically turn the pup's head toward you so

Do not let your frisky Dandie pull you down the street. Let him realize that the leash and collar mean school time.

you can bring him back easily to the heel position. Give quiet, reassuring praise every time the leash goes slack and he's staying with you.

Staying and heeling can take a lot out of a dog, so provide playtime and free-running exercise to shake off the stress when the lessons are over. You don't want him to associate training with all work and no fun.

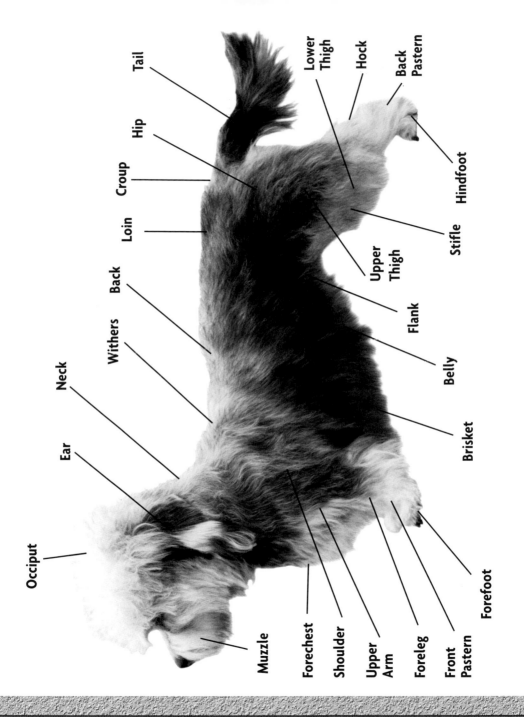

Tail

Lower Thigh

Hock

Back Pastern

Hip

Hindfoot

Croup

Loin

Stifle

Back

Upper Thigh

Withers

Flank

Neck

Belly

Ear

Brisket

Occiput

Muzzle

Forechest

Shoulder

Upper Arm

Foreleg

Front Pastern

Forefoot

PHYSICAL STRUCTURE OF THE DANDIE DINMONT TERRIER

DANDIE DINMONT TERRIER

By Lowell Ackerman DVM, DACVD

HEALTHCARE FOR A LIFETIME

When you own a dog, you become his healthcare advocate over his entire lifespan, as well as being the one to shoulder the financial burden of such care. Accordingly, it is worthwhile to focus on prevention rather than treatment, as you and your pet will both be happier.

Of course, the best place to have begun your program of preventive healthcare is with the initial purchase or adoption of your dog. There is no way of guaranteeing that your new furry friend is free of medical problems, but there are some things you can do to improve your odds. You certainly should have done adequate research into the Dandie and have selected your puppy carefully rather than buying on impulse. Health issues aside, a large number of pet abandonment and relinquishment cases arise from a mismatch between pet needs and owner expectations. This is entirely preventable with appropriate planning and finding a good breeder.

Regarding healthcare issues specifically, it is very difficult to make blanket statements about where to acquire a problem-free pet, but, again, a reputable breeder is your best bet. In an ideal situation you have the opportunity to see both parents, get references from other owners of the breeder's pups and see genetic-testing documentation for several generations of the litter's ancestors. At the very least, you must thoroughly investigate the Dandie Dinmont Terrier and the problems inherent in that breed, as well as the genetic testing available to screen for those problems. Genetic testing offers some important benefits, but testing is available for only a few disorders in a relatively small number of breeds and is not available for some of the most common genetic diseases, such as hip dysplasia, cataracts, epilepsy, cardiomyopathy, etc. This area of research is indeed exciting and increasingly important, and advances will continue to be made each year. In fact, recent research has shown that there is an equivalent dog gene for 75% of known human genes, so research done in either species is likely to benefit the other.

We've also discussed that evaluating the behavioral nature of your Dandie and that of his immediate family members is an

1. Esophagus
2. Lungs
3. Spleen
4. Liver
5. Stomach
6. Intestines
7. Urinary Bladder

INTERNAL ORGANS OF THE DANDIE DINMONT TERRIER

important part of the selection process that cannot be underestimated or overemphasized. It is sometimes difficult to evaluate temperament in puppies because certain behavioral tendencies, such as some forms of aggression, may not be immediately evident. More dogs are euthanized each year for behavioral reasons than for all medical conditions combined, so it is critical to take temperament issues seriously. Start with a well-balanced, friendly companion and put the time and effort into proper social-ization, and you will both be rewarded with a lifelong valued relationship.

Assuming that you have started off with a pup from healthy, sound stock, you then become responsible for helping your veterinarian keep your pet healthy. Some crucial things happen before you even bring your puppy home. Parasite control typically begins at two weeks of age, and vaccinations typically begin at six to eight weeks of age. A pre-pubertal evaluation is typically scheduled for about six months of age. At this time, a dental evaluation is done (since the adult teeth are now in), heartworm prevention is started and neutering or spaying is most commonly done.

It is critical to commence regular dental care at home if you have not already done so. It may not sound very important, but most dogs have active periodontal disease by four years of age if they don't have their teeth cleaned regularly at home, not just at their veterinary exams. Dental

> **DENTAL WARNING SIGNS**
> A veterinary dental exam is necessary if you notice one or any combination of the following in your dog:
> • Broken, loose or missing teeth
> • Loss of appetite (which could be due to mouth pain or illness caused by infection)
> • Gum abnormalities, including redness, swelling and bleeding
> • Drooling, with or without blood
> • Yellowing of the teeth or gumline, indicating tartar
> • Bad breath.

problems lead to more than just bad "doggy breath." Gum disease can have very serious medical consequences. If you start brushing your dog's teeth and using antiseptic rinses from a young age, your dog will be accustomed to it and will not resist. The results will be healthy dentition, which your pet will need to enjoy a long, healthy life.

Most dogs are considered adults at a year of age, although some larger breeds still have some filling out to do up to about two or so years old. Even individual dogs within each breed have different healthcare require-ments, so work with your veterinarian to determine what will be needed and what your role should be. This doctor-client relationship is important, because as vaccination guidelines change, there may not be an annual "vaccine visit" scheduled.

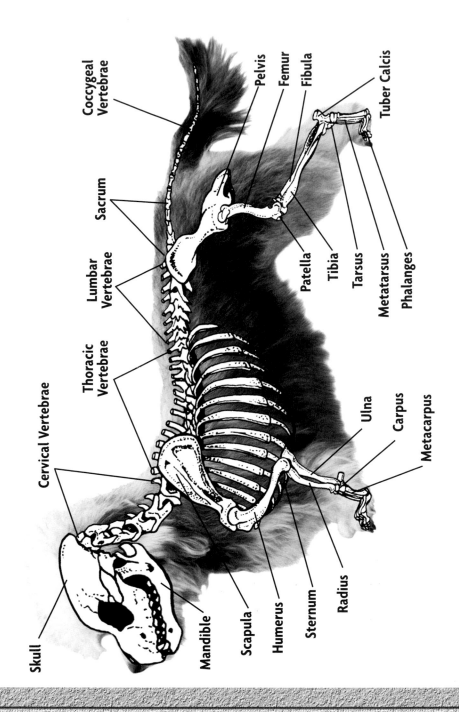

Coccygeal Vertebrae

Pelvis

Femur

Fibula

Tuber Calcis

Sacrum

Patella

Tibia

Tarsus

Metatarsus

Phalanges

Lumbar Vertebrae

Thoracic Vertebrae

Cervical Vertebrae

Ulna

Carpus

Metacarpus

Skull

Mandible

Scapula

Humerus

Sternum

Radius

Skeletal Structure of the Dandie Dinmont Terrier

You must make sure that you see your veterinarian at least annually, even if no vaccines are due, because this is the best opportunity to coordinate healthcare activities and to make sure that no medical issues creep by unaddressed.

When your Dandie reaches three-quarters of his anticipated lifespan, he is considered a "senior" and likely requires some special care. In general, if you've been taking great care of your canine companion throughout his formative and adult years, the transition to senior status should be a smooth one. Age is not a disease, and as long as everything is functioning as it should, there is no reason why most of late adulthood should not be rewarding for both you and your pet. This is especially true if you have tended to the details, such as regular veterinary visits, proper dental care, excellent nutrition and management of bone and joint issues.

At this stage in your Dandie's life, your veterinarian may want to schedule visits twice yearly, instead of once, to run some laboratory screenings, electrocardiograms and the like, and to change the diet to something more digestible. Catching problems early is the best way to manage them effectively. Treating the early stages of heart disease is so much easier than trying to intervene when there is more significant damage to the heart muscle. Similarly, managing the beginning of kidney problems is fairly routine if there is no significant kidney damage. Other problems, like cognitive dysfunction (similar to senility and Alzheimer's disease), cancer, diabetes and arthritis, are more common in older dogs, but all can be treated to help the dog live as many happy, comfortable years as possible. Just as in people, medical management is more effective (and less expensive) when you catch things early.

SELECTING A VETERINARIAN

There is probably no more important decision that you will make regarding

TAKING YOUR DOG'S TEMPERATURE

It is important to know how to take your dog's temperature at times when you think he may be ill. It's not the most enjoyable task, but it can be done without too much difficulty. It's easier with a helper, preferably someone with whom the dog is friendly, so that one of you can hold the dog while the other inserts the thermometer.

Before inserting the thermometer, coat the end with petroleum jelly. Insert the thermometer slowly and gently into the dog's rectum about one inch. Wait for the reading, about two minutes. Be sure to remove the thermometer carefully and clean it thoroughly after each use.

A dog's normal body temperature is between 100.5 and 102.5 degrees F. Immediate veterinary attention is required if the dog's temperature is below 99 or above 104 degrees F.

your pet's healthcare than the selection of his doctor. Your pet's veterinarian will be a pediatrician, family-practice physician and gerontologist, depending on the dog's life stage, and will be the individual who makes recommendations regarding issues such as when specialists need to be consulted, when diagnostic testing and/or therapeutic intervention is needed and when you will need to seek outside emergency and critical-care services. Your vet will act as your advocate and liaison throughout these processes.

Everyone has his own idea about what to look for in a vet, an individual who will play a big role in his dog's (and, of course, his own) life for many years to come. For some, it is the compassionate caregiver with whom they hope to develop a professional relationship to span the lifetime of their dogs and even their future pets. For others, they are seeking a clinician with keen diagnostic and therapeutic insight who can deliver state-of-the-art healthcare. Still others need a veterinary facility that is open evenings and weekends, is in close proximity or provides mobile veterinary services to accommodate their schedules; these people may not much mind that their dogs might see different veterinarians on each visit. Just as we have different reasons for selecting our own healthcare professionals (e.g., covered by insurance plan, expert in field, convenient location, etc.), we should not expect that there is a one-size-fits-all recommendation for selecting a veterinarian and veterinary practice. The best advice is to be honest in your assessment of what you expect from a veterinary practice and to conscien-

Your Dandie will really make himself at home.

tiously research the options in your area. You will quickly appreciate that not all veterinary practices are the same, and you will be happiest with one that truly meets your needs.

There is another point to be considered in the selection of veterinary services. Not that long ago, a single veterinarian would attempt to

Keep a close eye on your Dandie puppy when he's outdoors. Most puppies are as naughty as they are cute.

manage all medical and surgical issues as they arose. That was often problematic, because veterinarians are trained in many species and many diseases, and it was just impossible for general veterinary practitioners to be experts in every species, every breed, every field and every ailment. However, just as in the human healthcare fields, specialization has allowed general practitioners to concentrate on primary healthcare delivery, especially wellness and the prevention of infectious diseases, and to utilize a network of specialists to assist in the management of conditions that require specific expertise and experience. Thus there are now many types of veterinary specialists, including dermatologists, cardiologists, ophthalmologists, surgeons, internists, oncologists, neurologists, behaviorists, criticalists and others to help primary-care veterinarians deal with complicated medical challenges. In most cases, specialists see cases referred by primary-care veterinarians, make diagnoses and set up management plans. From there, the animals' ongoing care is returned to their primary-care veterinarians. This important team

PROBLEM: AND THAT STARTS WITH "P"

Urinary tract problems more commonly affect female dogs, especially those who have been spayed. The first sign that a urinary tract problem exists usually is a strong odor from the urine or an unusual color. Blood in the urine, known as hematuria, is another sign of an infection, related to cystitis, a bladder infection, bladder cancer or a blood-clotting disorder. Urinary tract problems can also be signaled by the dog's straining while urinating, experiencing pain during urination and genital discharge as well as excessive water intake and urination.

Excessive drinking, in and of itself, does not indicate a urinary tract problem. A dog who is drinking more than normal may have a kidney or liver problem, a hormonal disorder or diabetes mellitus. Behaviorists report a disorder known as psychogenic polydipsia, which manifests itself in excessive drinking and urination. If you notice your dog drinking much more than normal, take him to the vet.

HEARTWORM PREVENTIVES

There are many heartworm preventives on the market, many of which can be dispensed from your veterinarian's office. These products can be given daily or monthly, depending on the manufacturer's instructions. All of these preventives contain chemical vermicides directed at killing heartworms, which leads to some controversy among dog owners. In effect, heartworm preventives are necessary evils, though you should determine how necessary based on your pet's lifestyle. There is no doubt that heartworm is a dreadful disease that threatens the lives of dogs. However, the likelihood of your dog's being bitten by an infected mosquito is slim in most places, and a mosquito repellent (or an herbal remedy such as wormwood or black walnut) is much safer for your dog and will not compromise his immune system (the way heartworm preventives will). Should you decide to use the traditional preventive "medications," you can consider giving the pill every other or third month. Since the toxins in the pill will kill the heartworms at all stages of development, the pill would be effective killing larvae, nymphs or adults, and it takes four months for the larvae to reach the adult stage. Thus there is no rationale to poisoning the dog's system on a monthly basis. Lastly, do not give the pill during the winter months, since there are no mosquitoes around to pass on their infection, unless you live in a tropical or semi-tropical environment.

approach to your pet's medical-care needs has provided opportunities for advanced care and an unparalleled level of quality to be delivered.

With all of the opportunities for your Dandie to receive high-quality veterinary medical care, there is another topic that needs to be addressed at the same time—cost. It's been said that you can have excellent healthcare or inexpensive healthcare, but never both; this is as true in veterinary medicine as it is in human medicine. While veterinary costs are a fraction of what the same services cost in the human healthcare arena, it is still difficult to deal with unanticipated medical costs, especially since they can easily creep into hundreds or even thousands of dollars if specialists or emergency services become involved. However, there are ways of managing these risks. The easiest is to buy pet health insurance and realize that its foremost purpose is not to cover routine healthcare visits but rather to serve as an umbrella for those rainy days when your pet needs medical care and you don't want to worry about whether or not you can afford that care.

Pet insurance policies are very cost-effective (and very inexpensive by human health-insurance standards), but make sure that you buy the policy long before you intend to use it (preferably starting in puppyhood, because coverage will exclude pre-existing conditions) and that you are actually buying an indemnity insurance plan from an insurance company that is regulated by your state or province. Many insurance policy look-alikes are actually discount clubs that are redeemable only at specific locations and for specific services. An indemnity plan covers your pet at almost all veterinary, specialty and emergency practices and is an excellent way to manage your pet's ongoing healthcare needs.

COMMON INFECTIOUS DISEASES

Let's discuss some of the diseases that create the need for vaccination in the first place. Following are the major canine infectious diseases and a simple explanation of each.

Rabies: A devastating viral disease that can be fatal in dogs and people. In fact, vaccination of dogs and cats is an important public-health measure to create a resistant animal buffer population to protect people from contracting the disease. Vaccination schedules are determined on a government level and are not optional for pet owners; rabies vaccination is required by law in all 50 states.

Parvovirus: A severe, potentially life-threatening disease that is easily transmitted between dogs. There are four strains of the virus, but it is believed that there is significant "cross-protection" between strains that may be included in individual vaccines.

Distemper: A potentially severe and life-threatening disease with a relatively high risk of exposure, especially in certain regions. In very high-risk distemper environments, young pups may be vaccinated with human measles vaccine, a related virus that offers cross-protection when administered at four to ten weeks of age.

Hepatitis: Caused by canine adenovirus type 1 (CAV-1), but since vaccination with the causative virus has a higher rate of adverse effects, cross-protection is derived from the use of adenovirus type 2 (CAV-2), a cause of respiratory disease and one of the potential causes of canine cough. Vaccination with CAV-2 provides long-term immunity against hepatitis, but relatively less protection against respiratory infection.

Canine cough: Also called tracheobronchitis, actually a fairly complicated result of viral and bacterial offenders; therefore, even with vaccination, protection is incomplete. Wherever dogs congregate, canine cough will likely be spread among them. Intranasal vaccination with *Bordetella* and parainfluenza is the best safeguard, but the duration of immunity does not appear to be very long, typically a year at most. These are non-core vaccines, but vaccination is sometimes mandated by boarding kennels, obedience classes, dog shows and other places where dogs congregate to try to minimize spread of infection.

Leptospirosis: A potentially fatal disease that is more common in some geographic regions. It is capable of being spread to humans. The disease varies with the individual "serovar," or strain, of *Leptospira* involved. Since there does not appear to be much cross-protection between serovars, protection is only as good as the likelihood that the serovar in the vaccine is the same as the one in the pet's local environment. Problems with *Leptospira* vaccines are that protection does not last very long, side effects are not uncommon and a large percentage of dogs (perhaps 30%) may not respond to vaccination.

Borrelia burgdorferi: The cause of Lyme disease, the risk of which varies with the geographic area in which the pet lives and travels. Lyme disease is spread by deer ticks in the eastern US and western black-legged ticks in the western part of the country, and the risk of exposure is high in some regions. Lameness, fever and inappetence are most commonly seen in affected dogs. The extent of protection from the vaccine has not been conclusively demonstrated.

Coronavirus: This disease has a high risk of exposure, especially in areas where dogs congregate, but it typically causes only mild to moderate digestive upset (diarrhea, vomiting, etc.). Vaccines are available, but the duration of protection is believed to be relatively short and the effectiveness of the vaccine in preventing infection is considered low.

There are many other vaccinations available, including those for *Giardia* and canine adenovirus-1. While there may be some specific indications for their use, and local risk factors to be considered, they are not widely recommended for most dogs.

FLEA PREVENTION FOR YOUR DOG

- Discuss with your veterinarian the safest product to protect your dog, likely in the form of a monthly tablet or a liquid preparation placed on the back of the dog's neck.
- For dogs suffering from flea-bite dermatitis, a shampoo or topical insecticide treatment is required.
- Your lawn and property should be sprayed with an insecticide designed to kill fleas and ticks that lurk outdoors.
- Using a flea comb, check the dog's coat regularly for any signs of parasites.
- Practice good housekeeping. Vacuum floors, carpets and furniture regularly, especially in the areas that the dog frequents, and wash the dog's bedding weekly.
- Follow up house-cleaning with carpet shampoos and sprays to rid the house of fleas at all stages of development. Insect growth regulators are the safest option.

VACCINATIONS AND INFECTIOUS DISEASES

It is important to realize that whether or not to use a particular vaccine depends on the risk of contracting the disease against which it protects, the severity of the disease if it is contracted, the duration of immunity provided by the vaccine, the safety of the product and the needs of the individual animal. In a very general sense, rabies, distemper, hepatitis and parvovirus are considered core vaccine needs, while parainfluenza, *Bordetella bronchiseptica*, leptospirosis, coronavirus and borreliosis (Lyme disease) are considered non-core needs and best reserved for animals that demonstrate reasonable risk of contracting the diseases.

NEUTERING/SPAYING

Sterilization procedures (neutering for males/spaying for females) are meant to accomplish several purposes. While the underlying premise is to address the risk of pet overpopulation, there are also some medical and behavioral benefits to the surgeries as well. For females, spaying prior to the first estrus (heat cycle) leads to a marked reduction in the risk of mammary cancer. There also will be no manifestations of "heat" to attract male dogs and no bleeding in the house. For males, there is prevention of testicular cancer and a reduction in the risk of prostate problems. In both sexes there may be some limited reduction in aggressive behaviors toward other dogs, and some diminishing of urine marking, roaming and mounting.

One of the important considerations regarding neutering is that it is a surgical procedure. This sometimes gets lost in discussions of low-cost procedures and commoditization of the process. In females, spaying is specifically referred to as an ovariohysterectomy. In this procedure, a midline incision is made in the abdomen and the entire uterus and both ovaries are surgically removed.

While this is a major invasive surgical procedure, it usually has few complications, because it is typically performed on healthy young animals. However, it is major surgery, as any woman who has had a hysterectomy will attest.

In males, neutering has traditionally referred to castration, which involves the surgical removal of both testicles. While still a significant piece of surgery, there is not the abdominal exposure that is required in the female surgery. In addition, there is now a chemical sterilization option, in which a solution is injected into each testicle, leading to atrophy of the sperm-producing cells. This can typically be done under sedation rather than full anesthesia. This is a relatively new approach, and there are no long-term clinical studies yet available.

Neutering/spaying is typically done around six months of age at most veterinary hospitals, although techniques have been pioneered to perform the procedures in animals as young as eight weeks of age. In general, the surgeries on the very young animals are done for the specific reason of sterilizing them before they go to their new homes. This is done in some shelter hospitals for assurance that the animals will definitely not produce any pups. Otherwise, these organizations need to rely on owners to comply with their wishes to have the animals "altered" at a later date, something that does not always happen.

WORM-CONTROL GUIDELINES

- Practice sanitary habits with your dog and home.
- Clean up after your dog and don't let him sniff or eat other dogs' droppings.
- Control insects and fleas in the dog's environment. Fleas, lice, cockroaches, beetles, mice and rats can act as hosts for various worms.
- Prevent dogs from eating uncooked meat, raw poultry and dead animals.
- Keep dogs and children from playing in sand and soil.
- Kennel dogs on cement or gravel; avoid dirt runs.
- Administer heartworm preventives regularly.
- Have your vet examine your dog's stools at your annual visits.
- Select a boarding kennel carefully so as to avoid contamination from other dogs or an unsanitary environment.
- Prevent dogs from roaming. Obey local leash laws.

PHOTO BY CAROLINA BIOLOGICAL SUPPLY CO.

Ascarid *Rhabditis*

PHOTO BY CAROLINA BIOLOGICAL SUPPLY CO.

Hookworm *Ancylostoma caninum*

PHOTO BY TAM C. NGUYEN.

Tapeworm *Dipylidium caninum*

PHOTO BY TAM C. NGUYEN.

Heartworm *Dirofilaria immitis*

SHOWING YOUR

DANDIE DINMONT TERRIER

TRAINING A DANDIE PUPPY FOR THE SHOW RING
BY DR. EMMA GREENWAY

Ch. King's Mtn. Stuart Little, as a show puppy, giving great joy to his owner/handler, Sandra Pretari.

Having a great-looking puppy that has been sold to you as a potential show dog does not necessarily mean he will become one. The way you

choose to raise that puppy, combined with his genetically determined temperament traits, will determine whether your dog is going to enjoy the show ring. This brings me to an important point. There is nothing more unattractive than watching a Dandie being dragged reluctantly around the ring or held together by someone down on their knees who is holding the dog's tail and head in position. This happens, unfortunately, the world over—but it doesn't have to be this way.

FROM THE BEGINNING: SELECTING THE PUPPY

Whether you are a breeder or a purchaser it is important to examine the litter of puppies with a critical eye, looking at both conformation and temperament attributes. I like to assess puppies at 8 weeks and 12 weeks, and it is at this point I begin to decide which puppies are pets and which have show potential. Obvious faults such as incorrect bites, high-set and -carried tails, short bodies and monorchidism are all clear markers that a puppy is of pet quality. Very few litters contain puppies that are all show quality, and it is my belief as a breeder that if we are constantly striving to improve quality, then it is important that we only keep, show and breed from the very cream of a litter. This I know flies in the face of those who see the breeding of every Dandie bitch born as the only way to save the breed from extinction, but it has been my experience and observation that when such indiscriminate breeding has happened in other breeds the number of genetic issues has rocketed. Despite the hysteria over the breed's declining numbers worldwide, we are comparatively speaking blessed with relatively few genetic issues, and I think we should not lose sight of this.

As an example I will tell you about a recent litter of six. I selected three promising puppies, two bitches and a dog. The other three puppies were placed in pet homes and, although at least one of them certainly would have gained his title, I placed him anyway as he was still inferior to the three I felt most promising. I think the emphasis on producing an impressive number of champions can be a dangerous thing, as it can lead to diminishing quality for the sake of breed records. For this reason I resist the temptation to sell every puppy that could "finish" his title as a show dog.

Of the three puppies I selected one bitch was clearly the standout pick of the litter: she had a long, shapely body, a pretty head and beautiful easy movement. She was

also extremely responsive to people, gregarious and smart enough to learn basic commands very quickly. The other bitch puppy was equally pretty and had a very sweet temperament, but she was much more submissive yet stubborn. The dog had some outstanding physical qualities, but in the litter seemed quite reticent and a bit of a "loner." As you can

Ch. King's Mtn. Elsbeth Elfwish, nearly a year old with the author in the Winners Bitch Class at the Devon Dog Association show.

At six months of age, King's Mtn. Stuart Little, free-stacking in the Winners Dog Class for his handler, Sandra Pretari.

see from this description, all three had quite fundamentally different temperaments, and to make them into show dogs, a lot of time, effort and training must be put in. What you must also understand is that not every beautiful Dandie, no matter how much training you put in, can be made to enjoy the show ring, and it is my belief that these Dandies should not be shown, though this does not mean they cannot be used carefully within a breeding program. Indeed in the case of the litter described here, the sweet Dandie bitch clearly did not enjoy being shown. Despite endless hours of training, she would slink around the ring and do what was asked, but she was only truly happy when on her owner's lap. This bitch

has become a brood bitch in the breeding program, while her brother, once separated from his litter and given intensive human time and training, became a very happy human-focused puppy who loved show training and being shown, as did his sister. Both became easy champions.

TRAINING

By now I imagine you are wondering how you get your pretty, outgoing and friendly puppy to want to be a show dog. When I say "show dog," let me describe what I mean and what you are aiming to have your Dandie be able to do.

A true show dog, aside from being of great physical quality, must look happy and confident in the ring; he is, after all, a "performer" and should look as if he enjoys being on stage. He must show that he wants to be there with you and that you and he have a relationship doing this thing called "showing" together as a team. He must be able to walk on a loose lead with his tail carried in a happy position and not tucked between his legs, and ideally he should be able to stand in position with his legs set four-square, with his rear legs not under him. He should know how to stop and stand still both on the ground and for inspection on the table.

Training a puppy to be a show dog is fundamentally about you, the owner and handler, learning how to communicate with your dog. All dogs and puppies desperately want to please their owner and pack leader, and it is up to you to work out how to let your puppy know when he is doing something you want. Just as it takes time to school a child, it takes time for a puppy to understand the concepts you are trying to teach him, and how quickly he learns is in part a result of how good a teacher you are.

Just as we teach children to read by first teaching them the alphabet, then getting them to read small words, sentences and so on, the task of teaching puppies requires that we break up the lesson tasks into small, digestible and clear segments. This is how I do it.

SOCIALIZATION

The big wide world can be a very scary place for a puppy with 3-inch legs, and it is important from the very outset that you begin to get your puppy used to the noises and confusion of life: banging, flapping, crashes, cars, children, people, baby carriages, bikes, shopping centers and, of course, other dogs. The better accustomed your dog is to the world, the less scary and stressful it will be for him. Many puppies' initial reaction to new experiences is to back off, bark, try to hide behind your legs or run away. Being scared is normal, but it is important that your puppy is given the time and space to overcome his fear. For example, if you are out walking with your puppy on a leash and a garbage can falls down near your puppy and the puppy reacts with fear, stop and allow your puppy the time to gradually overcome his fear. As he becomes braver reward him with encouraging words. Don't pat your puppy or give him a food reward until he is showing signs of bravery. This way you reward the bravery, not the fear.

These days veterinarians encourage owners not to take their puppies out until fully vaccinated,

A young and attentive Ch. King's Mtn. Minnie Mouse, free stacking on the table for owner/handler Don Watkins.

Don Watkins, gaiting his six-month-old Ch. King's Mtn. Minnie Mouse at the specialty.

Step One: Teaching a word that means food

This lesson can be taught at any age, but I find that six weeks of age is the youngest puppies are able to respond. In my household I use the word "treaty," but any word will do; some people like the word "cookie" or "bicky."

I like to use what I call "plastic cheese," that is the processed sliced cheese that comes individually wrapped, but anything strong smelling and tasty is good.

Making sure your puppy is hungry, using just one slice, and only one slice, of cheese, call the puppy to you and literally at the same time that you give the puppy a little piece of the slice of cheese say the word "treaty." (Remember, you can use any food command here that you wish.) I keep doing this until the slice is finished, then I stop, as too much of a good thing gets boring. I play this little game every day for about a week and usually by the time the week is up the puppy has learned that "treaty" means special food. You can test how well the puppy knows this by whether he rushes toward you when you say the key word. When he does, be sure to reward him. Never tease your puppy by saying the word and not giving him the food. This will only prove to confuse the puppy and make him think you can't be relied upon.

and while this has great medical merit it can mean that puppies miss out on valuable socialization experiences during their most impressionable age. For this reason I would encourage you to take your puppy out in the car, to visit friends and even carry him around the park or shopping center on a regular basis so he can begin to get a sense of the world while feeling safe in your arms.

A historical win for the Dandie: Harry, Aust. Grand/Am. Ch. Hobergays Fineus Fogg, breaks the Best in Show record with his win under Helen Lee James at the 2006 Kings Kennel Club Show. Owners, Dr. Emma Greenway, Capt. Jean Heath and Dr. William H. Cosby, Jr.

BEST IN SHOW

KINGS
KENNEL CLUB

Step Two: Preparing the puppy for walking on a lead

When you are certain your puppy knows that "treaty" means special food, begin to make the game a little more complicated. In a nice big area inside or out, call the puppy to you and walk along and encourage the puppy to walk with you. To start, take only a few steps, then say your key word and at the same time bend down and give your puppy some cheese. Do not play this game for any more than five minutes. Just like a child, a puppy's concentration span is very short, and you want to keep the training fun. This exercise teaches your puppy that it is fun to walk beside you and makes the transition to leash training easy.

Step Three: Teaching the puppy to watch what you are doing

Begin this lesson by doing what you did in step one: give your puppy cheese and the "treaty" word at the same time. After a couple of times doing this, say the puppy's name, show him the cheese and then, making sure he is watching you, drop the cheese a little in front of him. Allow him to rush up and get the treat and then do it again: call his name, making sure he watches you throw the cheese, and allow him to pick it up. Do this for just one slice of cheese, then stop. Repeat this for two or three days for about five minutes each day.

On the fourth day repeat the procedure but throw the cheese a little to the side of him, alternating sides; this way the puppy has to concentrate on watching you to figure out where the cheese will be thrown. As the puppy gets better at

this game, begin to throw the cheese farther back and away from him so that the puppy has to run over to get the treat. Very quickly you will find the puppy looking at you excitedly waiting to see where you are going to throw the food. This lesson teaches the puppy that you are fun and interesting to watch.

Step Four: Teaching the puppy to stand back and away from you

By now your puppy is excited at the prospect of his special time with you. You are going to continue the throwing game, but you are going to start to throw the food well back and behind the puppy, whose natural instinct will be to rush to your feet and look up at you to see where the treat will be dropped. After a little while, the puppy will realize that if he stands at your feet looking at you, it is very hard to follow where the food is being thrown. When the puppy rushes to find a treat you have thrown, try to get his attention and throw another treat at him before he has time to

If you are seriously interested in Dandies, join your national Dandie Dinmont club and enjoy meeting people whose interests are similar to your own.

rush back to your feet. This will sometimes take several days of five-minute training lessons to achieve. Resist the temptation to make your training sessions longer; your puppy will learn, but it may take as long as three weeks. Each puppy's learning speed is unique.

Step Five: Teaching your puppy to "stop"

Now that your puppy stands well back from you looking to see where you are going to throw the treat, the next lesson is to teach your puppy what the word "stop" means.

A three-year-old Ch. King's Mtn. Mouse Trap, gaiting for the judge at Montgomery County Kennel Club.

Please remember that this lesson is only about teaching your puppy the concept of "stop." It is not a lesson about your puppy standing still with all his legs four-square as in the show ring. When you see your puppy standing well back from you and standing still, say the word "Stop" and use a corresponding hand or finger action. I generally hold up my index finger, but you can use any signal as long as you are consistent with its use. As soon as you have said the word and done the signal, come toward the puppy very quickly so as not to give him time to move and give him a treat. Now this lesson must be carried out very quickly, as puppies rarely stay still for more than a few seconds and, if you reward the puppy with a treat after he has taken a few steps toward you, the puppy will not have begun to learn what "stop"

VETERAN

Dandie Dinmont
Terrier Club
Of America
50th Anniversary
Specialty
2 OCTOBER 1982

means. If your puppy moves, don't give him a treat. Go back to playing the "throwing treats" game and try again a minute or two later.

This is one of the hardest things to teach a puppy, and it can often take many weeks of lesson games to get him to understand what you want. I had one puppy who was very slow to learn, but one day it was like a light bulb went on. He had just picked up the thrown treat and was beginning to move toward me, and I said "Stop." The puppy stopped mid-stride, legs everywhere—it was the funniest thing to see—but he did stop and I did reward him. From that point on his stopping became more and more

reliable, and over time his legs were increasingly in a correct position. He was so proud of himself that he wagged furiously every time I asked him to stop. It is this joy and enthusiasm that you must try to harness for the show ring. Some dogs will be better than others; some will have that extra something that makes them not just a good show dog but a spectacular one.

Step Six: Teaching pup to back up
Now that your dog stands back from you on command, it is useful to also teach him to back up. Being able to ask your dog to back up, i.e., walk backwards and then stop in a stacked position, is very useful in

the show ring where there may be little room and time to get your dog in position. Getting your dog to back up can also facilitate getting him to stand with his feet correctly positioned. Incorporated with the stop command, it can also mean that you can have him looking his absolute best in a short amount of time. Begin by playing the "treaty" game with your dog. Ask him to "stop," then slowly walk toward him and, as you get close, ask him to go "back." Keep repeating the word and as soon as the dog goes to move backwards—even by one step and even if it's sideways—reward the dog with a treat and verbal praise. Very quickly the dog will

perfect going back neatly, but it is important that you reward every effort and not just a perfect backward step. Once the dog goes backwards reasonably well, ask him to "stop," and then you take several steps back and away from him, continuing to use the word and signal for stop. If the dog remains stacked and stopped, go toward him after a few seconds and reward him with a treat and words of praise. Remember your Dandie Dinmont is trying really hard to understand you and do what you want (not easy for this bright little terrier). If he fails to do what you ask, it is usually because you have not been a good enough teacher.

Emma Greenway, working with future show puppies.

Ch. Pennywise Gambit with owner/handler Cathy Nelson.

Step Seven: Now that your dog stops, stands and goes back on command, it is time to put him on his lead

As you may have noticed up until now, at no time have I told you to put your dog on a lead. The reality of the show ring is that all dogs must wear a lead, but that does not mean that the lead should be necessary, or that it should be used as the only method of communication you have with your dog. You should be aiming to be able to show your dog without having to resort to yanking on the lead to get your dog to do or go where you want. Now that your dog knows a little about what you want, put him on a lead and take him out to different places.

Winning under Catherine Nelson, Ch. King's Mtn. Pixie Montizard, at 18 months of age, was Best in Sweepstakes at the 1997 national specialty.

Encourage the dog to walk with you by rewarding him frequently, use the word "treaty" as you give him food, and use lots of encouraging words and a friendly voice. Begin by only walking the dog a few steps at a time between rewards and gradually increase the time between rewards. Walk your dog on a very long loose lead and play the "treaty" game on lead. Begin to incorporate stopping and standing and always be lavish with treats and praise. Never tease your dog; you will see people at shows waving food up and down in front of their dog outside the ring and then put the food back in their pocket. All they are teaching their dog is that they cannot be trusted to do what they have promised.

Now you are nearly ready to take your dog to a dog show and show him.

THE HANDLER

Now that your dog knows what to do, it is important that you do your best to look and behave in a way that complements your dog.

Try to wear neat, smart clothing that complements your dog's color. Try not to wear highly patterned clothing that can distract the eye of the judge or conceal your Dandie's wonderful outline. Do not, if you are a woman, wear long and flapping skirts, which can be distracting to the dog and the judge. Wear flat and comfortable shoes. Always carry yourself with

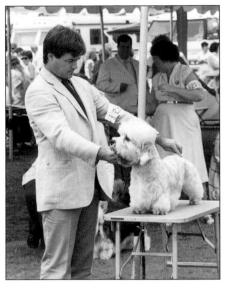

Ch. Sandon's Grey Poupon Deejon, handled by the late Brad Woolridge, in the specials ring at the Santa Barbara Kennel Club show.

confidence and pride, but remember it is your dog and not you that is on show.

Make sure you go to some dog shows and just watch how the ring procedure works and what handlers do. Pay particular attention to those dogs and handlers who look like

Ch. King's Mtn. Cordelia, handled by co-owner Miriam Couto, winning under Dick Yoho. Gail Isner is the trophy presenter.

they are a team and are having fun. Often you can pick up valuable clues as to how to handle better from watching the good, the bad and the ugly in the ring. Ask the good ones questions. If you get a chance, go to some handling classes.

Most of all, be prepared to lose and be gracious and polite whether you are a winner or a loser. Know that you are always taking the best dog home whether you win or lose.

Do not scold, chastise or punish your dog for misbehaving in the ring. If your dog didn't get the ring workout right, it might be because you haven't done a good enough job teaching him and making it fun. Also, your dog may be unwell or may have injured himself. Always remember that it is hard for a dog to look happy if you have just scolded him.

Ch. Pennywise King's Mtn. MVP was Best of Breed at the 1995 Dandie Dinmont Club of America's national specialty under judge Dr. Samuel Draper. Author Betty-Anne Stenmark is presenting the sterling silver bowl.

ENTER THE SHOW RING

Let's think about some basic questions:

- Did you purchase a "show-quality" puppy from the breeder?
- Is your puppy at least six months of age?
- Does the puppy exhibit correct show type for his breed?
- Does your puppy have any disqualifying faults?
- Is your Dandie registered with the American Kennel Club?
- How much time do you have to devote to training, grooming, conditioning and exhibiting your dog?
- Do you understand the rules and regulations of a dog show?
- Do you have time to learn how to show your dog properly?
- Do you have the financial resources to invest in showing your dog?
- Will you show the dog yourself or hire a professional handler?
- Do you have a vehicle that can accommodate your weekend trips to the dog shows?

Assuming that you have purchased a puppy of the correct type and quality for showing, let's begin to examine the world of showing and what's required to get started. Although the entry fee into a dog show is nominal, there are lots of other hidden costs involved with "finishing" your Dandie, that is, making him a champion. Things like equipment, travel, training and conditioning all cost money. A

FOR MORE INFORMATION...

For reliable up-to-date information about registration, dog shows and other canine competitions, contact one of the national registries by mail or via the Internet.

American Kennel Club
5580 Centerview Dr., Raleigh, NC 27606-3390
www.akc.org

United Kennel Club
100 E. Kilgore Road, Kalamazoo, MI 49002
www.ukcdogs.com

Canadian Kennel Club
89 Skyway Ave., Suite 100, Etobicoke, Ontario M9W 6R4, Canada
www.ckc.ca

The Kennel Club
1-5 Clarges St., Piccadilly, London W1Y 8AB, UK
www.the-kennel-club.org.uk

likely will catch the "bug." Once the dog-show bug bites, its effects can last a lifetime; it's certainly much better than a deer tick! Soon you will be envisioning yourself in the center ring at the Westminster Kennel Club Dog Show in New York City, competing for the prestigious Best in Show cup. This magical dog show is televised annually from Madison Square Garden, and the victorious dog becomes a celebrity overnight.

AKC CONFORMATION SHOWING

GETTING STARTED

As we've mentioned, visiting a dog show as a spectator is a great place to start. Pick up the show catalog to find out what time your breed is being shown, who is judging the breed and in which ring the classes will be held. To start, Dandies compete against other Dandies, and the winner is selected as Best of Breed by the judge. This is the

more serious campaign will include fees for a professional handler, boarding, cross-country travel and advertising. Top-winning show dogs can represent a very considerable investment—over $100,000 has been spent in campaigning some dogs. (The investment can be less, of course, for owners who don't use professional handlers.)

Many owners, on the other hand, enter their "average" Dandies in dog shows for the fun and enjoyment of it. Dog showing makes an absorbing hobby, with many rewards for dogs and owners alike. If you're having fun, meeting other people who share your interests and enjoying the overall experience, you

An 11-month-old King's Mtn. Elsbeth Elfwish on the move. Owned by Donna Francis and Sandra Wolfskill.

Ch. Pastime Rex Hairison, bred by Phil and Karen Cramer, owned by Pastime Dandies, won the Breed twice at Montgomery, 2001 and 2005.

procedure for each breed. At a group show, all of the Best of Breed winners go on to compete for Group One in their respective group. For example, all Best of Breed winners in a given group compete against each other; this is done for all seven groups. Finally, all seven group winners go head to head in the ring for the Best in Show award.

What most spectators don't understand is the basic idea of conformation. A dog show is often referred as a "conformation" show. This means that the judge should decide how each dog stacks up (conforms) to the breed standard for his given breed: how well does this Dandie conform to the ideal representative detailed in the standard? Ideally, this is what happens. In reality, however, this ideal often gets slighted as the judge compares Dandie #1 to Dandie #2. Again, the ideal is that each dog is judged based on his merits in comparison to his breed standard, not in comparison to the other dogs in the ring. It is easier for judges to compare dogs of the same breed to decide which they think is the better specimen; in the Group and Best in Show ring, however, it is very difficult to compare one breed to another, like apples to oranges. Thus the dog's conformation to the breed standard—not to mention advertising dollars and good handling—is essential to success in conformation shows. The dog described in the standard (the standard for each AKC breed is written and approved by the breed's national parent club and then submitted to the AKC for approval) is the perfect dog of that breed, and breeders keep their eye on the standard when they choose which dogs to breed, hoping to get closer and closer to the ideal with each litter.

Another good first step for the novice is to join a dog club. You will be astonished by the many and different kinds of dog clubs in the country, with about 5,000 clubs holding events every year. Most clubs require that prospective new members present two letters of recommendation from existing members. Perhaps you've made some friends visiting a show held by a particular club and you would like to join that club. Dog clubs may specialize in a single breed, like a local or regional Dandie club, or in a specific pursuit, such as obedience, tracking or hunting tests. There are all-breed clubs for all-dog enthusiasts; they sponsor special training days, seminars on topics like grooming or handling or lectures on breeding or canine genetics. There are also clubs that specialize in certain types of dogs, like herding dogs, hunting dogs, companion dogs, etc.

A parent club is the national organization, sanctioned by the American Kennel Club, which

The judge's first glance at a line-up of show Dandies.

promotes and safeguards its breed in the country. The Dandie Club of America was formed in 1932 and can be contacted on the Internet at http//clubs.akc.org/ddtca. The parent club holds an annual national specialty show, usually in a different city each year, in which many of the country's top dogs, handlers and breeders gather to compete. At a specialty show, only members of a single breed are invited to participate. There are also Group specialties, in which all members of a Group are invited. The Terrier Group has the most famous show—the Montgomery County Kennel Club. For more information about dog clubs in your area, contact the American Kennel Club at www.akc.org on the Internet or write them at their Raleigh, NC address.

HOW SHOWS ARE ORGANIZED

Three kinds of conformation shows are offered by the AKC. There is the all-breed show, in which all AKC-recognized breeds can compete; the specialty show, which is for one breed only and usually sponsored by the breed's parent club and the group show, for all breeds in one of the AKC's seven groups. The Dandie competes in the Terrier Group.

For a dog to become an AKC champion of record, the dog must earn 15 points at shows. The points must be awarded by at least three different judges and must include two "majors" under different judges. A "major" is a three-, four- or five-point win, and the number of points per win is determined by the number of dogs competing in the show on that day. (Dogs that are absent or are excused are not counted.) The number of points that are awarded varies from breed to breed. More dogs are needed to attain a major in more popular breeds, and fewer dogs are needed in less popular breeds. Yearly, the AKC evaluates the number of dogs in competition in each division (there are 14 divisions in all, based on geography) and may or may not change the numbers of dogs required for each number of points. For example, a major in Division 2

Groomed and ready...look as snazzy and prepared as your Dandie does!

(Delaware, New Jersey and Pennsylvania) recently required 17 dogs or 16 bitches for a three-point major, 29 dogs or 27 bitches for a four-point major and 51 dogs or 46 bitches for a five-point major. The Dandie attracts numerically proportionate representation at all-breed shows.

Only one dog and one bitch of each breed can win points at a given show. There are no "co-ed" classes except for champions of record. Dogs and bitches do not compete against each other until they are champions. Dogs that are not champions (referred to as "class dogs") compete in one of five classes. The class in which a dog is entered depends on age and previous show wins. First there is the Puppy Class (sometimes divided further into classes for 6- to 9-month-olds and 9- to 12-month-olds); next is the Novice Class (for dogs that have no points toward their championship and whose only first-place wins have come in the Puppy Class or the Novice Class, the latter class limited to three first places); then there is the American-bred Class (for dogs bred in the US); the Bred-by-Exhibitor Class (for dogs handled by their breeders or by immediate family members of their breeders) and the Open Class (for any non-champions). Any dog may enter the Open Class, regardless of age or win history, but to be competitive the dog should be older and have ring experience.

The judge at the show begins judging the male dogs in the Puppy Class(es) and proceeds through the other classes. The judge awards first through fourth place in each class. The first-place winners of each class then compete with one another in the Winners Class to determine Winners Dog. The judge then starts over with the bitches, beginning with the Puppy Class(es) and proceeding up to the Winners Class to award Winners Bitch, just as he did with the dogs. A Reserve Winners Dog and Reserve Winners Bitch are also selected; they could be awarded the points in the case of a disqualification.

The Winners Dog and Winners Bitch are the two that are awarded the points for their breed. They then go on to compete with any champions of record (often called "specials") of their breed that are entered in the show. The champions may be dogs or bitches; in this class, all are shown together. The judge reviews the Winners Dog and Winners Bitch along with all of the champions to select the Best of Breed winner. The Best of Winners is selected between the Winners Dog and Winners Bitch; if one of these two is selected Best of Breed as well, he or she is automatically determined Best of Winners. Lastly, the judge selects Best of Opposite Sex to the Best of Breed winner. The Best of Breed winner then goes on to the Group competition.

At a Group or all-breed show, the Best of Breed winners from each breed are divided into their respective groups to compete against one another for Group One through Group Four. Group One (first place) is awarded to the dog that best lives up to the ideal for his breed as described in the standard. A Group judge, therefore, must have a thorough working knowledge of many breed standards. After placements have been made in each Group, the seven Group One winners (from the Sporting Group, Toy Group, Hound Group, etc.) compete against each other for the top honor, Best in Show.

There are different ways to find out about dog shows in your area. The American Kennel Club's monthly magazine, the *American Kennel Gazette* is accompanied by, the *Events Calendar*; this magazine is available through subscription. You can also look on the AKC's and your parent club's websites for information and check the event listings in your local newspaper.

Your Dandie must be six months of age or older and registered with the AKC in order to be entered in AKC-sanctioned shows in which there are classes for the Dandie. Your Dandie also must not possess any disqualifying faults and must be sexually intact. The reason for the latter is simple: dog shows are the proving grounds to determine which dogs and bitches are worthy of being bred. If they cannot be bred, that defeats the purpose! On that note, only dogs that have achieved championships, thus proving their excellent quality, should be bred. If you have spayed or neutered your dog, however, there are many AKC events other than conformation, such as obedience trials, agility trials and the Canine Good Citizen® Program, in which you and your Dandie can participate.

OTHER TYPES OF COMPETITION
In addition to conformation shows, the AKC holds a variety of other competitive events. Obedience trials, agility trials and tracking trials are open to all breeds, while hunting tests, field trials, lure coursing, herding tests and trials, earthdog tests and coonhound events are limited to specific breeds or groups of breeds. The Junior Showmanship program is offered to aspiring young handlers and their dogs, and the Canine Good Citizen® Program is an all-around good-behavior test open to all dogs, pure-bred and mixed.

OBEDIENCE TRIALS
Any dog registered with the AKC, regardless of neutering or other disqualifications that would preclude entry in conformation competition, can participate in obedience trials.

There are three levels of difficulty in obedience competition. The first (and easiest) level is the

Novice, in which dogs can earn the Companion Dog (CD) title. The intermediate level is the Open level, in which the Companion Dog Excellent (CDX) title is awarded. The advanced level is the Utility level, in which dogs compete for the Utility Dog (UD) title. Classes at each level are further divided into "A" and "B," with "A" for beginners and "B" for those with more experience. In order to win a title at a given level, a dog must earn three "legs." A "leg" is accomplished when a dog scores 170 or higher (200 is a perfect score). The scoring system gets a little trickier when you understand that a dog must score more than 50% of the points available for each exercise in order to actually earn the points. Available points for each exercise range between 20 and 40.

A dog must complete different exercises at each level of obedience. The Novice exercises are the easiest, with the Open and finally the Utility levels progressing in difficulty. Examples of Novice exercises are on- and off-lead heeling, a figure-8 pattern, performing a recall (or come), long sit and long down and standing for examination. In the Open level, the Novice-level exercises are required again, but this time without a leash and for longer durations. In addition, the dog must clear a broad jump, retrieve over a jump and drop on recall. In the Utility level, the exercises are quite

difficult, including executing basic commands based on hand signals, following a complex heeling pattern, locating articles based on scent discrimination and completing jumps at the handler's direction.

Once he's earned the UD title, a dog can go on to win the prestigious title of Utility Dog Excellent (UDX) by winning "legs" in ten shows. Additionally, Utility Dogs who win "legs" in Open B and Utility B earn points toward the lofty title of Obedience Trial Champion (OTCh.). Established in 1977 by the AKC, this title requires a dog to earn 100 points as well as three first places in a combination of Open B and Utility B classes under three different judges. The "brass ring" of obedience competition is the AKC's National Obedience Invitational. This is an exclusive competition for only the cream of the obedience crop. In order to qualify for the

Coming through the tunnel is Ch. Windsedge Joie of Dunsandle, VCDI, RN, CG, owned by France Roozen and Richard Yoho.

Ch. Windsedge Joie of Dunsandle, VCDI, RN, CG, over the jump. She is the most titled agility Dandie in the sport. Owners, France Roozen and Richard Yoho.

invitational, a dog must be ranked in either the top 25 all-breeds in obedience or in the top three for his breed in obedience. The title at stake here is that of National Obedience Champion (NOC).

AGILITY TRIALS

Agility trials became sanctioned by the AKC in August 1994, when the first licensed agility trials were held. Since that time, agility certainly has grown in popularity by leaps and bounds, literally! The AKC allows all registered breeds (including Miscellaneous Class breeds) to participate, providing the dog is 12 months of age or older. Agility is designed so that the handler demonstrates how well the dog can work at his side. The handler directs his dog through, over, under and around an obstacle course that includes jumps, tires, the dog walk, weave poles, pipe tunnels, collapsed tunnels and more. While working his way through the course, the dog must keep one eye and ear on the handler and the rest of his body on the course. The handler runs along with the dog, giving verbal and hand signals to guide the dog through the course.

The first organization to promote agility trials in the US was the United States Dog Agility Association, Inc. (USDAA). Established in 1986, the USDAA sparked the formation of many member clubs around the country. To participate in USDAA trials, dogs must be at least 18 months of age.

Agility trials are a great way to keep your dog active, and they will keep you running, too! You should join a local agility club to learn more about the sport. These clubs offer sessions in which you can introduce your dog to the various obstacles as well as training classes to prepare him for competition. In no time, your dog will be climbing A-frames, crossing the dog walk and flying over hurdles, all with you right beside him. Your heart will leap every time your dog jumps through the hoop—and you'll be having just as much (if not more) fun!

TRACKING

Tracking tests are exciting ways to test your Dandie's instinctive scenting ability on a competitive level. All dogs have a nose, and all breeds are welcome in tracking tests. The first AKC-licensed tracking test took place in 1937 as part of the Utility level at an obedience trial, and thus competitive tracking was officially begun. The first title, Tracking Dog (TD), was offered in 1947, ten years after the first official tracking test. It was not until 1980 that the AKC added the title Tracking Dog Excellent (TDX), which was followed by the title Versatile Surface Tracking (VST) in 1995. Champion Tracker (CT) is awarded to a dog who has earned all three of those titles.

Successfully tracking the leather glove, Ch. Kamlo's Raise'N A Rumpus, UD, TD, owned and trained by Mrs. Lee Palmer.

Lee Palmer with "Rumpus", bred by Dora Ortwein and Karen Dorn.

Can. Ch. Torcroft Young Bess, the breed's first Certificate of Gameness winner, at an AWTA trial, getting set to make her history-making run in the author's arms.

Bess enters the den at an AWTA trial, on her way to her CG.

EARTHDOG EVENTS

The American Working Terrier Association (AWTA) began holding tests for terriers in the early 1970s and awarded the Certificate of Gameness (CG) to qualifying dogs. The author and her Can. Ch. Torcroft Young Bess were the first Dandie team to win a CG.

Earthdog trials are held for those breeds that were developed to "go to ground." These dogs were bred to go down into badger and fox holes and bring out the quarry. Breeds such as Parson Russell

The TD level is the first and most basic level in tracking, progressing in difficulty to the TDX and then the VST. A dog must follow a track laid by a human 30 to 120 minutes prior in order to earn the TD title. The track is about 500 yards long and contains up to 5 directional changes. At the next level, the TDX, the dog must follow a 3- to 5-hour-old track over a course that is up to 1,000 yards long and has up to 7 directional changes. In the most difficult level, the VST, the track is up to 5 hours old and located in an urban setting.

Terriers, Dachshunds and other short-legged hunters are used in this fashion. Earthdog trials test the dog in a simulated hunting situation in which trenches are dug and lined, usually with wood. The scent of a rat is laid in the trench, and the quarry is a caged rat at the end of the tunnel. The dog can see and smell the rat but cannot touch or harm the quarry in any way.

Bess has worked the quarry for the required amount of time and is about to be pulled out of the den. Success!

There are four levels in earthdog trials. The first, Introduction to Quarry, is for beginners and uses a 10-foot tunnel. No title is awarded at this level. The Junior Earthdog (JE) title is awarded at the next level, which uses a 30-foot tunnel with three 90-degree turns. Two qualifying JE runs are required for a dog to earn the title. The next level, Senior Earthdog (SE), uses the same length tunnel and number of turns as in the JE level, but also has a false den and exit and requires the dog to come out of the tunnel when called. To try for the SE title, a dog must have at least his JE; the SE title requires three qualifying runs at this level. The most difficult of the earthdog tests, Master Earthdog (ME), again uses the 30-foot tunnel with three 90-degree turns, with a false entrance, exit and den. The dog is required to enter in the right place and, in this test, honor another working dog. The ME title requires four qualifying runs, and a dog must have earned his SE title to attempt the ME level.

Little Bess and Jiminy Kricket working the quarry on King's Mtn.

INDEX

My Dandie Dinmont Terrier

PUT YOUR PUPPY'S FIRST PICTURE HERE

Dog's Name _____

Date _____ Photographer _____